CLIFTON E. OLMSTEAD is Professor of Religion and
Executive Officer of the Department of Religion at
The George Washington University. The author of
*History of Religion in the United States,* he is also a
contributor to *The World Book Encyclopedia* and is
a lecturer on religion for the U.S. Department of
State.

*Maul Holsinger*
1962

# RELIGION IN AMERICA

# RELIGION IN AMERICA
# PAST AND PRESENT
# CLIFTON E. OLMSTEAD

A SPECTRUM BOOK

PRENTICE-HALL, INC.

ENGLEWOOD CLIFFS, N.J.

PRINTED IN THE UNITED STATES OF AMERICA

77322-C

To Mother

# Preface

History, we are told, is the recreation of the past for the enrichment of the present. It is fashioned out of the warp and woof of human experience; and into its rich tapestry are interwoven the strands of hope and fear, of dream and disillusion, revealing our kinship with past generations.

When men have pondered deeply the meaning of existence, they have invariably sought fellowship with a power greater than their own which might inform and guide them through the fluctuating currents of temporal incertitude. In this way religion has joined the interplay of forces which affect the cultural process. Historically, it has given evidence of its potency in a host of societies, not the least of which has been the relatively young and burgeoning entity known as the United States. It is that complex and diversified phenomenon known as American religion with which this book purposes to deal.

# Table of Contents

# RELIGION IN AMERICA

CHAPTER ONE

# The Old World Heritage

That perceptive French visitor, Tocqueville, wrote in 1831: "America is the only country in which it has been possible to witness the natural and tranquil growth of society, and where the influences exercised on the future condition of states by their origin is clearly distinguishable." His observation is instructive. American society, in its evolution, bore the obvious marks of a dynamic encounter between an Old World heritage and a New World environment. In no area of human experience is this judgment more applicable than in the realm of religious thought and life.

Over a period of 350 years, the religious heritage of Old Europe was adapted, molded, and assimilated on the American continent. Out of a seeming welter of heterogeneous and often conflicting ideologies, there emerged a faith which, although it still carried the imprint of its European ancestry, was uniquely American. Thus the saga of American religion is one of metamorphosis. In this chapter we shall review the major spiritual forces in sixteenth-century Europe which served as catalytic agents in the American religious process.

## THE RIGHT WING OF THE REFORMATION

As a religious movement, the Protestant Reformation of the sixteenth century took as its common characteristic the rejection of the authority of the Roman Church. In the minds of its leaders, this action, deemed necessary after repeated failures to win reform, constituted no schism from the church. It was rather a schism in the church. The Reformers claimed to be heirs of the church's Biblical and patristic heritage. They appealed to Jesus Christ himself for their authority and taught that God's redemptive activity was final in him. They conceived Christianity as an individual matter between the soul and God, grounded in the act of redemption and sustained by the inner presence of the Holy

1

Spirit. Such an individualistic doctrine necessarily would lead ultimately to a variety of formal religious expressions, thus accounting for a diversity of denominations and sects in the Protestant tradition.

For the most part, the earliest products of the Reformation were great churchly systems which retained a Catholic sense of the church even though they broke with Rome. Closely allied with strong nationalistic forces in their countries, they were invariably accorded the privileges pertaining to an establishment. These systems, which belonged to the right wing of the Reformation, were the Lutheran, the Reformed, the Anglican, and with some justification, the Puritan.

While the Reformation was precipitated by Martin Luther's historic theses of 1517 on the misuse of indulgences, its mature development depended upon the treatment of more vital issues. Luther (1483-1546) met this need in his three treatises of 1520, which defined the essence of Protestant faith. In *The Address to the Christian Nobility of the German Nation* he asserted the right of the civil power to reform the church. Attacking the exalted state of the clergy, he argued that every baptized Christian is a priest. Since all persons had immediate access to God through faith, the spiritual privileges of the clergy could not exceed those of the laity. In *The Babylonian Captivity of the Church* he maintained that only the sacraments of baptism, the Lord's Supper, and possibly penance could be justified on the basis of the New Testament. In *The Freedom of a Christian Man* he taught the doctrine of justification by faith; through this justification the righteousness of Christ was imputed to man as his own righteousness. By faith, Luther meant the unquestioning acceptance of the Gospel, a trust of the heart and commitment of the will, resulting in a joyous reconciliation with God and bearing fruit in righteous works.

Luther was reluctant to break with the church and refrained from taking this step until he realized that the fundamental disparities between the Roman system and his own were too great to permit reconciliation. By the mid-1520's, all Germany was divided into Lutheran and Catholic camps. The movement soon spread into the Scandinavian countries, where Lutheranism became the state religion.

Another important work of reformation was begun in Geneva, Switzerland, in 1536, with the arrival of John Calvin (1509-1564), a French refugee. At the pinnacle of his theological system, recorded in the *Institutes of the Christian Religion*, stood the doctrine of God as absolute sovereign will. God not only brought all things into being but maintains them through every moment of their existence. Because of total depravity, man is unable to do God's will or to work out his own salvation. But God is merciful and in His providence He elects some men to eternal life. Men cannot know of a certainty that they are numbered among the elect; yet, if they respond to the witness of the Holy Spirit and lead righteous lives, this may be an indication of election.

God's way of accomplishing His will on earth is through the elect, who are appointed to carry out His plan. They do this by applying the doctrines and commandments of the Bible to every detail of life. Thus while Calvin was pessimistic in his view of natural man, he was optimistic in his view of history. Wherever his doctrines were carried—France, the Lowlands, Scotland, England, the colonies—the attempt was made to transform society according to what Calvinists believed to be the will of God.

In England, the Reformation was at first chiefly political and liturgical; doctrinal and ethical problems which troubled Luther and Calvin were given only secondary importance. A recasting of Catholic doctrine was certainly not intended by Henry VIII, nor did he reject any part of Roman teaching, except the papal claim to universal jurisdiction. Political motives at one point prompted Henry to enter into friendly relations with the Protestant princes of Germany. This is reflected in the Ten Articles of 1536, which emphasized justification by faith and affirmed only three sacraments. But a reaction soon set in and in 1539, the Six Articles, decidedly conservative and Catholic in character, were issued.

With the accession of Edward VI in 1547, the government came under the aegis of the Protestant party and significant reforms were put into effect. Two monumental contributions made under the guidance of Thomas Cranmer (1489-1556), Archbishop of Canterbury, were the Book of Common Prayer and the Forty-two Articles. In 1571, the articles were pruned to Thirty-nine, their present form. The articles emphasized those things on which the Continental reformers agreed.

In the latter half of the sixteenth century the Puritan movement began as an agitation within the Church of England. Puritans stood for the conviction that the church should be restored to the simplicity and purity of the first-century fellowship and that reforms in England were thus far inadequate. They saw the observance of Christmas and the use of the cross and priestly vestments as innovations of Romanism which were to be abhorred. In 1603, they drew up a formal list of abuses in the Millenary Petition. James I granted only one request: the production of the celebrated Authorized Version of the Bible.

At the heart of the Puritan system was the Federal theology, grounded in Calvinism, which stressed the covenant relationship between God and man. The effect was to place more emphasis on the role of man in salvation, since a covenant has no value unless two parties accept it. In the areas of society and government Puritan thought followed Calvinism; society's chief purpose was to do the will of God. Since natural man was sinful, it followed that God's will could be done only if government were in the hands of the holy and regenerate (those who held Puritan views).

## THE LEFT WING OF THE REFORMATION

Almost simultaneously with the rise of the great churchly systems of Protestantism there arose a number of religious groups or schools of thought which gave full expression to the divisive and individualistic tendencies latent within the Reformation. They were generally built around some particular emphasis which members of the fellowship believed to be expressive of the essence of Christianity. Protestants of the left wing conceived the church as a fellowship rather than an organization and deemed a soul-searching personal decision prerequisite to communicant membership. Their forms of polity were simple, usually of the congregational type. Although they gradually assumed a more churchly character, they never aspired to become church establishments. Their strength lay in the piety of their adherents and the strictness of their discipline. Their influence was deeply felt in Europe, and in America their religious character and type became normative.

In the first stage of the Reformation, the most numerous and influential followers of left-wing Protestantism in Germany and Switzerland were called Anabaptists or Rebaptizers. They held that the church, since it is the community of saints composed of true believers alone, could not be co-extensive with the state. Into the true church they would receive only those persons who gave evidence in character and conduct of having been regenerated, accepting Christ publicly and receiving believers' baptism. Infant baptism was repudiated, since baptism was only a symbol of regeneration which had already taken place in the believer. A cardinal tenet of the Anabaptists was the complete separation of church and state. Experience had taught them that where such a union existed persecution of dissenting groups invariably followed. It was their conviction that physical compulsion could not properly be exercised in matters of faith. By the end of the Reformation period, Anabaptism had crystallized into a number of denominations such as the Mennonites, Baptists, and Moravians.

In addition to the Puritans, who believed in the union of church and state, there was a smaller group in England, the Separatists, whose theology was essentially Puritan but whose polity was quite different. Their principles were set forth chiefly by Robert Browne (1550-1633), who taught that the church is merely a local company of Christians who freely enter into a covenant with God and with one another and who carry on their Christian life and work as a united fellowship. Wherever redeemed persons enter into such a covenant, there is a true church. This idea became one of the fundamental principles of the Congregational churches. Browne did not consider infant baptism a sacrament, but accepted it on the ground that children ought to be dedicated to God and the church. Those who could not agree withdrew and founded what were to become the English Baptist churches.

While the main stream of the Reformation moved toward a careful systematization of doctrine and polity, another branch stressed the importance of the mystical experience or inner light. George Fox (1624-1691), founder of the movement in its English phase, preached the possibility of direct enlightenment through the influence of the Holy Spirit. He and his followers, who were called Friends or Quakers, believed that the illuminating power of the Holy Spirit is conferred on all men and is not limited to truth already received through Scripture. Since all men were equally dependent on the Spirit, all persons should be equal in the church. No clergy were necessary, for the Spirit would inspire persons in the congregation to speak concerning their experience. The Friends came to be known for a dominant spirit of Christian kindness and an absolute condemnation of war.

## THE ROMAN CATHOLIC COUNTER-REFORMATION

Despite significant losses suffered by the Roman Church as a result of the Protestant Reformation, it sustained enough vitality to stage a remarkable recovery. To accomplish this, however, the church had to meet two needs. The first was to take the mass of medieval doctrine and tradition and weld it into a carefully defined doctrinal system. This was accomplished at the Council of Trent, a general council which met intermittently from 1545 to 1563 at Trent, in the Austrian Tyrol.

The council declared that the body of revealed truth for Christians was to be found not only in the Bible, as maintained by the Protestants, but also in the unwritten tradition of Christ's teaching, preserved by the church under the guidance of the Holy Spirit. Concerning the doctrine of salvation, the council held that the sinner is justified by the merits of Christ, if they produce merits in him, so that he obeys the commandments of God and the church. It was further taught that the seven sacraments are necessary to salvation.

Some noteworthy practical reforms were also accomplished at Trent. Provision was made for more adequate supervision of clerical morals and for improved education of the clergy. Priests were ordered to expound the Scriptures in the larger towns and to see that everywhere the people were taught in a lucid way the essential articles of faith.

The second need of the Roman Church was an aggressive movement to promote its ideas and practices and to impede the progress of Protestantism. Such a movement was found in the order known as the Society of Jesus, which originated in the mind of a Spanish priest, Ignatius Loyola (1491-1556). At the University of Paris, in 1528-1529, Loyola gathered a small band of disciples who were to pledge themselves to the special service of the pope. In 1540, they were officially recognized as the Society of Jesus. The Jesuit order was an officers' corps, designed to lead everywhere in the work of the Roman Church, notably in missions, education, and diplomacy. The general of the order was supreme dictator, subject only to the pope.

The Jesuits contributed greatly to the strengthening of the papacy, particularly to the movement which culminated in the infallibility decree of 1870. They fostered secondary and higher education, founding universities wherever they went. They won new lands for the church, soon becoming the supreme missionary order. Their influence in America was potent, both in the Spanish missions of the South and Southwest and in the French missions in the Northeast and Mississippi Valley.

CHAPTER TWO

# Church and Empire
# in Colonial America

## THE MISSIONS OF NEW SPAIN

Almost a century before the English colonization of Virginia, Roman Catholic Spain was planting permanent settlements within the borders of what is now the United States. Perhaps no nation entered the American forest primeval with more vigor and enthusiasm and sense of mission. Certainly none was able to blend more effectively its economic, political, and religious goals in a comprehensive and unified program for colonization.

In June, 1526, two Dominican priests and a lay-brother sailed with Lucas Vásquez de Ayllón for America. They began a settlement on the Chesapeake near the future site of Jamestown, and it was probably there that the first mass within the present borders of the United States was celebrated. Within a year, only a minority of the settlers survived, and these returned home in dejection.

The first permanent Spanish settlement in Florida was inspired by antipathy for a French Huguenot colony which was established in that territory in 1562. Three years later Pedro Menéndez de Avilés attacked and destroyed the settlement, fortified the peninsula, and called it St. Augustine. A number of Jesuits soon took up residence there, while a larger group labored as far north as the Chesapeake. After this mission failed, the work was taken up by Franciscans who, by 1634, were conducting forty-four missions. But with success came a spirit of complacency, resulting in laxity and perfunctory service on the part of the missionaries. Efforts at reform were made, but they were neither penetrating nor permanent.

Meanwhile, interest in the exploration of interior America had

7

developed, and soldiers and missionaries were following the trails which led to the vast unknown West. The year 1541 found de Soto at the Mississippi and Coronado in southern Nebraska, each promoting the missionary cause as much as possible, but with modest and impermanent results. In 1597, another expedition proceeded up the Rio Grande; a settlement was made at San Juan de los Caballeros, and mass was celebrated in the first church edifice to be completed in New Mexico. As in Florida, the missionaries were superficially successful in winning converts to the faith. Yet there soon evolved a spirit of complacency among the ecclesiastical leaders, who were often more concerned with exploiting the free labor of the Indian than with improving his immediate spiritual welfare. The result was an Indian uprising in 1680, in which half of the clergy and 400 white settlers lost their lives. Not until 1700 did the province again enjoy relative peace.

With the advent of the eighteenth century, Spanish power and influence in the East entered a period of eclipse. From 1763 to 1783, Florida was under English domination, during which time the Spanish missionaries found progress difficult. Though Florida reverted to Spain in 1783, the political tensions continued until 1819, when the Spanish government ceded it to the United States.

In New Mexico, the eighteenth century brought decline and decay to Spanish Christianity. Religion was popularly an object either of indifference or hatred. By 1845, there were only seventeen priests left in the province. Three years later New Mexico became a part of the United States and the Spanish-Mexican rule was ended.

The Spanish mission movement in Texas dates predominantly from the early eighteenth century, with the founding of the San Antonio de Valero, Concepcion, and San Jose missions. The work of settlement, however, did not prosper since the Spanish government regarded Texas as little more than a field on which to deter French aggression. By the close of the eighteenth century, there were scarcely 7000 whites in the entire area, but in the 1820's, large numbers of Americans moved into Texas. During these confused times, when Mexico was winning independence from Spain and territorial lines were almost constantly shifting, friction between Americans and Mexicans increased, finally leading to revolt, the creation of a new republic, and its annexation in 1845 to the United States.

Among the more colorful of the Spanish missions were those of California. In 1769, a settlement was established at San Diego and the Franciscan missionary, Father Junípero Serra, founded the mission of San Diego de Alcala, the first in a chain of Franciscan missions. He founded eight other missions before his death in 1784, among them San Gabriel, San Antonio, and San Juan Capistrano.

The mission, because of its economic and political as well as religious significance, proved to be the most effective institution of Hispanic control. It did much more than spread the faith; it served as dispenser of Spanish culture and civilization. Its task was unusually difficult due to the radical cultural inferiority of the Indians. They had to be taught advanced methods in agriculture, building, and the domestic arts, and encouraged to work at various trades. Some efforts were made toward the intellectual enrichment of the natives, but it seemed impossible to impart more than the basic doctrines considered essential to the salvation of their souls.

The collapse of Spanish authority in Mexico in 1821 prompted the shift of California's loyalty to the new Mexican government the following year. For the missions this marked the beginning of ruin. Mexican politicians, during the years 1834 to 1840, confiscated the mission lands, removed the friars, and introduced secular priests who had relatively little interest in the progress of the Indians. Thus collapsed the work of sixty-five years, a work which had led to the baptism of 100,000 aborigines.

In assaying the ultimate worth of the Spanish missions it is easy to be critical. The clerics, like the soldiery, were agents of the Spanish crown and were thoroughly imbued with the love of empire. On occasions that passion subverted the noblest Christian ideals so that the Indian was more manipulated than marshaled. At the same time, the Spaniard regarded the Indian as a backward neighbor who needed to be prepared for a richer life in community. Thus the Spanish policy was to assimilate the aboriginal stock in race, religion, and culture. The result was a new civilization in which Spanish and Indian elements fused. To this day the great Southwest bears the cultural imprint of that historic encounter.

## THE MISSIONS OF NEW FRANCE

If France was somewhat tardier than Spain in planting permanent settlements in America, the delay could not be charged to want of vision. She was fully cognizant of the remarkable opportunities which the New World presented. But being preoccupied with domestic problems, she found it impossible to make significant progress in the colonization enterprise until the seventeenth century.

The first missionary efforts by French Roman Catholics within the present borders of the United States came in direct answer to a felt challenge. By 1640, the Jesuits had erected five chapels among the Hurons west of Montreal and had baptized more than 100 natives. Their work, however, was rendered extremely hazardous by the frequent raids of the Iroquois, the bitterest enemies of the Hurons. In 1642, Father Isaac Jogues sought to bring Christianity to the Iroquois in what is now the state of New York. They captured him and subjected him to the tortures of burning and mutilation. Though he escaped in 1643, he returned three years later to win the martyr's crown.

A decade later, the wily Iroquois, having encountered opposition from other tribes to the south and west, found it beneficial to sign a treaty with the French and allow a mission to be set up among the Onondagas in central New York. For a time six priests worked with these duplicitous natives, but their efforts came to naught. The English occupied New York and incited the Iroquois against the French. So successful were the English in gaining their purposes that by 1687 the French felt obliged to abandon their permanent posts in Iroquois territory. With that action, local Jesuit activity came to a virtual halt.

Meanwhile, new opportunities were opening in the West. For some years the majestic St. Lawrence had been luring French explorers into the vast, mysterious interior. Close behind had come the Jesuit missionaries, one of the most colorful of whom was Father Jacques Marquette, founder of St. Ignace mission at the mouth of Lake Michigan in 1670. He joined forces with the adventurer, Louis Joliet, and together, in 1673, they began a journey down the Mississippi, which they explored to its juncture with the Arkansas. Within a few years Jesuit and Récollet priests were conducting missions in this vast area.

By the opening of the eighteenth century, it was becoming apparent that the French government regarded New France not so much as an enterprise for trade and evangelism as a base of operations against the English. The lower Mississippi Basin and the Gulf Plains soon became the scene of a bitter contest for power. There was similar development farther to the north. In western Illinois, where missions had been established at Cahokia in 1699 and Kaskaskia in 1700, permanent settlements and forts were built by 1720. At each of these places the church continued its ministrations, but there was a singular absence of the piety which had characterized the seventeenth-century missionaries. Even the missions reflected the secular interests of the age.

At the outbreak of the French and Indian War, there were only one Récollet, eleven Sulpician, and thirty-eight Jesuit priests in all of New France. Clearly, a minority of these dwelt within the present borders of the United States. With the fall of Quebec and Montreal, an English victory was assured. According to the terms of the Paris treaty of 1763, France ceded to Great Britain, Canada and all its territory east of the Mississippi, while New Orleans went with Louisiana to Spain. The French population in the West never overcame its enmity for the

British; and when the Revolution broke out, it wholeheartedly supported the American side.

The trait which made the work of the French missionaries unique was the ability to blend their lives with those whom they sought to serve. If the Spanish played the role of mildly indulgent fathers in a family of wayward children, the French acted as brothers who won their status by deeds of kindness and courage. They were no more effective than the Spanish in impressing upon the Indian consciousness the fuller implications of their faith. At best they were able to apply a thin and impermanent veneer of Christian idealism to a primitive culture, somewhat resentful of the intrusion. Still the missionaries achieved some remarkable feats. The very fact that centuries after the collapse of French power in Northeast America, Roman Catholicism has flourished in Quebec is indicative of a powerful and abiding clerical influence.

## THE COMING OF THE ANGLICANS

The founding of the first permanent English colony in Virginia and the planting of the Church of England in America were synchronous events. In 1606, James I granted a charter to the London Company to found a colony in the territory of Virginia. Its immediate purposes were to seek out mineral deposits, to investigate agricultural and industrial possibilities, and to discover the northwest passage to the Orient. The settlers were to be accorded all the rights and privileges of Englishmen at home, among them the services of the Established Church. In the spring of 1607, a tiny settlement was begun at Jamestown and the first Holy Communion upon Virginia soil was celebrated by Robert Hunt, an Anglican clergyman. Captain John Smith had this to say about subsequent services:

> I well remember wee did hang an awning (which is an old saile) to three or foure trees to shadow us from the Sunne, our walles were rales of wood, our seats unhewed trees till we cut plankes, our Pulpit a bar of wood nailed to two neighboring trees. In foule weather we shifted into an old rotten tent. . . . Yet wee had daily Common Prayer morning and evening, every Sunday two Sermons and every three moneths the holy Communion, till our Minister died.[1]

With the founding of the Jamestown settlement there began a steady process pointing toward the creation of a church establishment. In 1619,

[1] P. G. Mode, *Sourcebook and Bibliographical Guide for American Church History* (Banta, c.1921), 10.

the Virginia Assembly enacted a number of laws relative to the practice of religion. Among them were provisions which not only required all ministers to conduct services of worship in accordance with the usage of the Church of England, but also compelled all persons to attend divine service twice on Sundays on pain of fine or bodily punishment.

Under the administration of Governor William Berkeley who arrived in 1641, there was a decided promotion of the church establishment. Ministers had to certify that they were episcopally ordained and pledge themselves to conformity. Tithes for the support of the clergy were made a legal requirement of the citizenry, and no person outside the Church of England was permitted suffrage. In 1641, the Assembly passed an act creating vestries for the government of the parishes; in each parish there should be twelve vestrymen elected by the voters of the parish. After 1662, the vestries chose their own successors, thus enabling them to keep their own class in power.

The size of the parishes was dictated by the geographical distribution of the population. Jamestown, the chief center of the colony, could scarcely be thought of as a real town. Most of the population was settled on extensive plantations paralleling the river banks. This necessitated the creation of parishes so many miles long that clergymen could not properly care for them. That attendance at divine worship was irregular was not surprising. Few had the perseverance to travel fifteen miles or more over ill-conditioned roads to participate in public worship, even in balmy weather. The problem was lessened to a degree by the establishment of chapels in remote areas; but where such chapels were lacking, ministers were sometimes obliged to travel to the homes of their parishioners and conduct what amounted to a private service.

One of the perennial problems was the raising of sufficient salaries for the clergy. In 1662, the Assembly passed an act making uniform all clerical salaries. The stipend was fixed at eighty pounds, the taxpayer being permitted to make his payment in tobacco. By this time, the market value of tobacco had declined sharply due to the navigation acts which forbade its shipment to foreign countries. When the clergy complained that their payments were inadequate to meet the rising costs of living, the assessments were increased. But the stipends were never adequate.

If the clergy were constantly harassed by poverty, they were outraged by the treatment they received from the vestries. No clergyman had life tenure in his parish unless his vestry presented him to the governor for induction or installation. On occasion, when a minister was regarded as exceptionally capable, the vestry would present him to the governor, but probably not more than one-tenth of the pastors ever received such an honor. This situation encouraged the abler ministers to remain in England, leaving the colonial pulpits staffed with mediocre divines.

In the proprietary colony of Maryland, first settled in 1634, the relation of the Anglican Church to the state was unusual. The charter granted to Cecil Calvert, Lord Baltimore, provided for the organization of churches according to the ecclesiastical laws of England, which meant the Anglican Church. Lord Baltimore, however, was a Roman Catholic; and part of his motivation in founding the colony was to seek a refuge for persecuted fellow-Catholics. Thus it happened that there were Jesuit priests but no Anglican clergy to minister to the needs of the citizenry, the larger percentage of whom were Protestants. The first Anglican clergyman did not arrive until about 1650.

With the overthrow of James II in 1688, a revolt was touched off in Maryland in which the Roman Catholic proprietor lost his power. The province was then made over into a royal colony under the immediate control of the Assembly, which was composed of Protestants. The policy of toleration was brought to an end, and the Assembly took steps to bring about the establishment of the Church of England.

The religion of the average Anglican in Virginia or Maryland might be characterized as pious but not prudish, formal but not fastidious. He believed in his religion and endeavored to practice it, without at the same time making it the foremost consideration of his life. His piety was evident in his choice of reading matter, in his public observances, in his laws. Most private libraries included one or more popular works on the practice of religion; thanksgiving days and "days of humiliation" belonged as much to Virginia as to New England; the regulations for the keeping of the Sabbath read like a page out of a Puritan law book. For all his outward professions of piety, however, the colonial Anglican often treated the ordinances of the church with reverent neglect. If a phlegmatic settler happened to drift into the local tavern when he was supposed to be in church, few were eager to chastise him. The easy-going plantation life admitted a tolerance unknown to a more disciplined society.

How successful the first settlers were in communicating their faith to the Indians we do not know. Probably there was no organized missionary work during the earliest years due to incessant warfare; but by 1617, the Virginia settlers were making plans for the founding of churches and schools for the Indians, eventually even a college. Then came the Indian massacre of 1622, an event which permanently soured the colonists on mission work. Henceforth they were devoted to the destruction of the Indian settlements.

Another challenge to the program of evangelism came with the intro-

duction of the Negro into the colonies. As early as 1619, twenty in-
dentured Negroes were landed in Virginia. The Negro proved to be
such an effective worker in the fields that the system of indenture
gradually evolved into slavery. As for the Negro's spiritual development,
there were probably few instances in which instruction was given in
Christian morals and doctrine. By 1680, the trend was to regard the
Negro as racially inferior and discriminate against him on that ground.

As the seventeenth century drew to a close, the Anglican Church in
Virginia was in a perilous condition. A majority of the parishes were
vacant; the minority were staffed by men of secondary ability. With
parishes too large to permit an effective ministry, out of clerical frustration had grown lethargy. Possibly no more than one person in
twenty was a member of the church.

Since there was no Anglican bishop in America during the colonial
period, the colonists had to look to the Bishop of London for episcopal
supervision. Such an arrangement left much to be desired and contributed
indirectly to the sorry state of church administration in America. To
Henry Compton, who became bishop in 1675, it was apparent that a
direct representative was needed who could act with authority. The
result was the appointment in 1689 of James Blair as first commissary to
the colony of Virginia. Blair was given powers of supervision and administration, but did not have the episcopal power to administer confirmation and ordination.

Commissary Blair, a man who commanded the respect of both secular
and clerical officialdom, began the work of reform by calling for higher
clerical salaries; but it was not until 1696 that legislation to meet this
need was approved by the governor. Perhaps Blair's most important
contribution was the founding of the College of William and Mary in
1693, the second college in the English colonies. Also noteworthy was his
ability to recruit clergy. By the time of his death in 1743, only two
parishes were without ministers.

A second commissary was Thomas Bray, appointed to Maryland in
1696. He is best known for his efforts in founding the "Society for the
Promotion of Christian Knowledge" in 1698 and the "Society for the
Propagation of the Gospel in Foreign Parts" in 1701. The principal
function of the latter was to further the ministrations of the Gospel
among English colonials and to evangelize the Indians and Negro slaves.
The Society's most important work, however, would be accomplished in
colonies other than Virginia or Maryland.

In 1663, Charles II granted a royal patent to eight proprietors for
lands south of Virginia, which were called Carolina. Dissenters as well
as Anglicans were drawn to the new colony, and every year there was a

considerable increase in the population. By 1706, the Anglican Church had been raised to the status of an establishment.

Georgia, founded in 1732 by Colonel James Oglethorpe, was a philanthropic venture on behalf of imprisoned debtors. Absorbed in this humanitarian enterprise, the proprietors freely granted religious liberty to all Christians save Roman Catholics. To the colony in its early days came the young John Wesley, then an Anglican missionary. Due to his unbending manner and uncompromising discipline, his tenure was cut short and he returned home to find his destiny. He was succeeded by George Whitefield, who would also win fame during the Great Awakening. In 1752, Georgia became a crown colony, and six years later an act was passed establishing the Anglican Church. Nevertheless, the Anglican Church in Georgia failed to prosper, a circumstance which existed through the remainder of the colonial period.

The only colony north of Maryland where there came to be anything resembling an Anglican establishment was New York, where Dutch rule was replaced by English in 1664. In 1693, the Assembly passed a bill which was later interpreted by the governors as establishing the Anglican Church in New York City and its neighboring counties. It is highly doubtful, however, if this was the intent of those who voted for the act. The document provided that the parishes should be served by a "good sufficient Protestant minister," a phrase which, in English legal usage, meant a clergyman of the Church of England. Doubtless this meaning was not understood by the Dutch members of the Assembly who voted for it. Not until 1697 was an Anglican parish founded in New York.

The growth of the Anglican Church in Pennsylvania, New Jersey, and the New England colonies was effected largely through the zealous functioning of missionaries sent by the Society for the Propagation of the Gospel. In the Middle Colonies they seem to have enjoyed some success in winning Quakers to their fold. In New England the Anglican missionaries encountered strong opposition from the Puritan leaders, and it was not until the second quarter of the eighteenth century that they were able to make any significant gains.

It seems ironical that the Anglican Church in the colonies found its greatest disadvantage in the assistance proffered by its proponent, the English government. In the South, where the church enjoyed the questionable benefits pertaining to an establishment, spiritual lethargy developed with unfailing regularity. Men of the highest ability and ideals could seldom be persuaded to accept a call to servility and uncertain tenure, subject to the whims of a vestry. There were notable exceptions, but not enough to place the clergy generally in a commanding position of respect. In New England, where Anglicans were a despised minority, their support by the English crown rendered them even more suspect. The more vigorously the government prosecuted their claims, the more public resentment was aroused. The saving feature of the church was the Society for the Propagation of the Gospel, with its band of consecrated missionaries working against overwhelming odds to advance the faith.

A constant source of frustration was the absence of a colonial episcopate. Without the benefit of either confirmation or ordination on this side of the Atlantic, the church could not possibly assume its normal function. This thought failed to excite any real concern in the South, where clergy and laity alike enjoyed the freedom from episcopal interference. In the Middle Colonies and New England determined efforts were made by missionaries and their congregations to have a bishop appointed, but all were doomed to failure. The church would have no bishop in America until after the formation of a national government, independent of England.

## EARLY DUTCH AND SWEDISH ESTABLISHMENTS

Torn by a long and bitter struggle with the Spanish which seriously depopulated their country, and preoccupied with trading concerns in the East, the Dutch had been slow to develop interest in American colonization. This situation began to change after Henry Hudson, in 1609, made his celebrated discovery of the river which bears his name. Mounting interest led to the organization of the Dutch West India Company in 1621; three years later the company sent over thirty Dutch and Walloon families to Fort Orange (Albany) and the Delaware. In 1626, Peter Minuit, soon to become the company's director, purchased Manhattan Island from the Indians and named it New Amsterdam.

The founders of New Netherland were men of enterprising bent, whose principal end in colonization was the acquisition of wealth. But reared in the established church of Holland, which was Calvinistic, they had developed a strong attachment to its faith and worship. They quite naturally, therefore, provided for the establishment of the Reformed religion in the new colony and took steps to institute services of worship. In 1628, the first Reformed minister, Domine Jonas Michaelius, arrived at Manhattan and organized a church. He was replaced in 1633 by Domine Everardus Bogardus.

One of the most colorful of the early ministers was Domine Johannes Megapolensis, who arrived in 1642 and labored for six years near Albany. He learned the Mohawk language and preached effectively to the Indians, being more successful with them than with his own people. He found the colonists indifferent to the ordinances of religion; they would sleep through his sermons and then spend the remainder of the Sabbath drinking and carousing.

The principal threat to the security of the colony and its church lay in the irresponsible policies of its directors and the mercenary considerations of the company which they represented. Receiving neither protection nor encouragement from the homeland, the colony was forced to struggle along as best it could. It was not until the coming of Peter Stuyvesant in 1647 that the colony's affairs took a turn for the better.

With the arrival of Director Stuyvesant, the colony began to thrive, and for a time a policy of toleration toward dissenters was maintained. Gradually Stuyvesant imposed more restrictions, and it became evident that he stood for religious exclusiveness. In 1654, he forbade the Lutherans on Manhattan Island to call a clergyman of their faith. Despite an enjoiner from the West India Company to treat the Lutherans mildly, Stuyvesant embarked on a campaign of persecution which led to the fining and imprisonment of nonconformists. None felt the weight of oppression more keenly than the Friends. Shortly after the arrival of their first missionaries, in 1657, two were imprisoned for preaching unauthorized doctrines in the streets. Three others, going on to Long Island, were apprehended and deported to Rhode Island. To this action, the Dutch Reformed clergy gave their full approval.

In the meantime, a band of Jews had landed on Manhattan Island in 1654. These Sephardic Jews, originating in Spain and Portugal, had taken refuge from their European persecutors in northern Brazil, which for a time was in the possession of the more tolerant Dutch. When the territory reverted to Portugal in 1654, they fled to New Amsterdam. Stuyvesant urged their deportation, but the West India Company intervened and granted them the rights of settlers. During the eighteenth century, they were joined by more of their brethren together with a few Ashkenazic Jews who had originated in Germany and Poland.

In September, 1664, Peter Stuyvesant, without a struggle, turned New Amsterdam over to the threatening English forces. The colony was renamed New York and the Dutch Reformed establishment was brought to an end. Any fears the Dutch might have had concerning the fate of their ministers and churches were dispelled by the surrender agreement, which provided that they should enjoy freedom of worship. The English had nothing to lose by the arrangement since they were then scarcely in a position to create an Anglican establishment in a colony which was predominantly Dutch. Even years later, after a bill of establishment had been enacted, they continued their policy of toleration toward the Dutch Church.

The dominant position of the Dutch continued throughout the

colonial period despite intermittent but ineffectual efforts on the part of the governors to advance the cause of Anglicanism or to take charge of the Dutch churches. The most serious obstacle to the Reformed churches was not the English government; it was an inflated sense of complacency. Not until the outset of the Great Awakening would the churches be jolted out of their lethargy; even then rigid formalists would sally forth to do battle with the besieging forces of enthusiasm.

As in the case of the Dutch, the motivation of the Swedes in colonization was economic. In 1638, two Swedish vessels sailed up the Delaware River to the present site of Wilmington and founded Fort Christina as a trading post. The ordinances of the Lutheran Church, the established church of Sweden, were made available in New Sweden with the arrival of Reorus Torkillus in 1639. To his successor, Johan Campanius, who arrived in 1643, went the honor of building the first Lutheran church on the island of Tinicum, near the present site of Essington, Pennsylvania. Campanius ministered to both whites and Indians. So great was his concern for the aborigines that he mastered the Delaware language and made a translation of Luther's Small Catechism.

When New Sweden fell to the Dutch in 1655, there were three Lutheran ministers in the colony. One was permitted to remain and conduct services for his Lutheran parishioners. This arrangement continued when the colony was taken over by the English nine years later. The Swedish Lutheran churches, nevertheless, remained virtually in a static condition until 1697, when the Archbishop of Uppsala sent three clergymen to the Delaware. For some years, the Swedish Lutheran churches thrived, especially during the ministry of Charles Magnus Wrangel which lasted from 1759 to 1768. Gradually, however, the Swedes became absorbed into their English environment and most of their congregations eventually affiliated with the Anglican Church.

CHAPTER THREE

# Puritan Beginnings
# in New England

By the opening of the seventeenth century, English Puritanism was moving rapidly toward crystallization. It recognized the Church of England, but as a loose federation of congregations, each receiving its authority direct from God. Moreover, it expected that these congregations would be unified through the support of the state. Thus the civil government would be responsible for the enforcement of church and civil law based upon the Scriptures and the suppression of all heretical movements. Only one major obstacle blocked the realization of this cherished plan: the hostility of the government under James I. When it became apparent that governmental opposition was increasing and that there was little prospect for the establishment of Puritanism in England, a saddened and despairing minority would seek ultimate victory through emigration.

## THE PILGRIMS OF PLYMOUTH

Meanwhile, a division in the Puritan ranks had resulted in the formation of the Separatist movement under the leadership of Robert Browne (1550-1633). Though sympathetic to the Puritan cause in many respects, Browne could not tolerate the existence of an established church. He conceived the church to be nothing more than a company of Christians who make a covenant with God and with one another and who labor together for the advancement of mutual Christian purposes. Wherever redeemed persons effected a covenant, giving evidence of a satisfactory conversion experience and of election to salvation, there was a true church.

The democratic organization of the Separatist churches called

19

for church officers to be chosen by and responsible to the entire con-gregation. Later, when the mantle of Separatist authority fell upon Henry Barrowe, the principle was changed so that power in a local church rested not with the membership but with the pastor, elders, and teachers. Browne's congregational democracy had been replaced by a modified Presbyterianism. Many years later John Cotton in New England would deny any connection with either Browne or Barrowe. Nevertheless, Browne's idea of the congregational covenant and Bar-rowe's concept of the eldership became realized in the church polity of Massachusetts Bay Colony.

The English government's persecution of the Separatists was vigorous, and many were forced to leave the country. In 1608, a congregation of Separatists, under the pastoral leadership of John Robinson, found asylum in Leyden. But the people did not feel at home in Holland; and when they heard reports of colonization in America, their interests turned in that direction. Finally, in 1620, their hopes were realized through the formation of a joint-stock company with all profits during the first seven years being equally divided between the settlers and the financiers. James I was suspicious of the Separatists, but since their settlement promised to provide much-needed raw materials, he grudg-ingly gave consent to the enterprise.

In July 1620, the Pilgrims departed for Southampton, whence they would journey to America. Since John Robinson remained behind, William Brewster (c.1566-1644), a ruling elder, became the spiritual leader of the adventurers. After weeks of delay, the Mayflower set sail; on November 11 the crew dropped anchor in Cape Cod Harbor. There the Separatist majority, fearing trouble from the non-Separatists on board and desiring some basis for a stable government, drew up a docu-ment known as the Mayflower Compact. It was the first step by Amer-ican colonists in the direction of framing a constitution or fundamental law.

There was almost constant tension with the London financiers. Having no real interest in the religious inclinations of the Separatists, they sought to people the colony with young men, irrespective of denomina-tional affiliation, who would be economically most productive. They even had the temerity to send as the first minister an Anglican clergyman; he was expelled from the colony. It was not until 1629 that a Separatist minister, Ralph Smith, arrived in Plymouth. His presence offered en-couragement to the Separatist element which was finding it increasingly difficult to hold the colony to its religious foundation and, with Gov-ernor William Bradford, was bemoaning the fact that "so many wicked persons and profane people should so quickly come over."

Despite the inroads made by non-Separatists, Plymouth Colony remained relatively free of theological controversy. Part of the reason lay in the fact that the Brownists, because of doctrinal and social inclinations, did not have the same admiration for education as did the Puritans. Men with a university education, such as Brewster, were few though highly influential in shaping public opinion.

Worship was designedly simple and unadorned with pageantry, the main parts being prayer and the reading and exposition of Scripture All "popish" observances, such as the celebration of Christmas, were soundly condemned. But the Pilgrims were not without diversion. Their observance of Thanksgiving Day, intended for the glorification of God, was marked by feasting and entertainment.

With the establishment of Massachusetts Bay Colony and the rapid influx of Puritan settlers during the 1630's, Plymouth looked to the newer Puritan colony for most of its gains in population. For some time the Plymouth colonists endeavored to obtain a separate royal charter but, failing in this, were obliged in 1691 to accept incorporation with Massachusetts.

## THE SWARMING OF THE PURITANS

In the meantime, the Puritans in the mother country were undergoing the severest disabilities. James I, ever more militant in his opposition to Puritanism, forced through Parliament in 1621 measures which required that baptized persons be confirmed by bishops and that they observe the festivals of Catholic Christianity. Charles I, who succeeded him in 1625, proved impossible. At the insistence of William Laud (1573-1645), the strong-willed Archbishop of Canterbury, Charles harshly enforced religious uniformity and thus found himself in conflict with the House of Commons. During these critical years, many Puritans made the decision to come to America; those who remained prepared the way for civil war.

As early as 1623, a group of Dorchester businessmen had founded a fishing company with base of operations at Gloucester. When the company failed, the Puritan minister of Dorchester, John White, conceived a plan whereby the settlement might become a haven for the poor and a center of missionary activity. It was taken up by a group of prominent Puritans who organized the New England Company. The history of Massachusetts Bay Colony begins with the arrival at Salem of their agent, John Endicott, and his followers in 1628. During the next twelve years some 20,000 colonists would follow Endicott to New England. Only a minority would be Puritans, but the control of the colony would be in their hands.

A charter incorporating the Massachusetts Bay Company was granted in 1629 by Charles I. It, of course, had nothing to say about matters ecclesiastical. Nevertheless, the company did make provision for ministerial support and decreed that "convenient churches" should be built. The settlers were permitted to choose their mode of church government.

In the spring of 1629, two non-Separatist Puritan ministers, Samuel Skelton and Francis Higginson, arrived at Salem and within a few months had organized a church with a congregational polity. The congregation adopted a Confession of Faith and a Covenant, then proceeded to ordain Skelton as pastor and Higginson as teacher, although both had received episcopal ordination. Thus was born the first non-Separatist church in America to be governed by congregational polity.

The Puritans and their Pilgrim confreres at Plymouth differed not only in their attitudes toward the church establishment but also in their views concerning the monarchy. The Puritans preferred to have a state without a monarch; the Pilgrims totally rejected the Anglican Church but gave full allegiance to their sovereign. This dissimilarity was sharply delineated in a remark attributed to Francis Higginson as he set sail from England:

> We do not go to New England as Separatists from the Church of England; though we cannot but separate from the corruptions in it, but we go to practise the positive part of church reformation and propagate the gospel in America.[1]

The "positive part of church reformation" did not include toleration. In their first confession of faith, the Massachusetts Puritans included an article which banned all diversity and conferred certain powers upon magistrates in matters of religion. A definite step in the direction of church establishment was taken by the first General Court in May 1631. At that session 110 people applied for admission as "Freemen." They took the oath of allegiance; but the court, fearing the outcome of so many people being given the franchise, decided that "noe man shall be admitted to the freedome of this body politicke, but such as are members of some of the Churches within the lymitts of the same." This ruling was justified by the court on the ground that government should remain in the hands of "honest and good men." According to legislation enacted in 1646, the failure to attend services of worship was punishable by a fine of five shillings; to reject any of the books of the Bible could result in whipping or even banishment.

While the colony purported to be a Christian state, the government was not by the clergy. To be sure, the ministers of the establishment

[1] Cotton Mather, *Magnalia Christi Americana* (Hartford, 1855), I, 362.

could not help but attain a wide influence in community life. Their advice was generally the best available in the colony, but they had no official role in government. The magistrates, on the other hand, did have official powers over the congregations, and they used them to the full limit of their office.

The continuing pressure of immigration together with the strait-laced policies of the Puritan authorities persuaded many settlers to seek their fortunes in another colony. Not all who left Massachusetts were discontented with the prevailing situation; clearly that was the case with the founders of New Haven. Most of the newer Puritan colonies, however, could trace their origins to some religious or political altercation in Massachusetts. The settlers fanned out along the coast and the inland waterways, establishing such colonies as Connecticut, New Hampshire, and New Haven, even migrating to the northern coast of Long Island and New Jersey.

## RELIGIOUS THOUGHT AND LIFE

The theology of the New England Puritans was basically the modified Calvinism of the English dissenters; it was expressed through such standards as the Westminster Confession, adopted by the Cambridge Synod in 1648, and the Savoy Confession, adopted by a synod of the churches in 1679. Its roots were in the Bible, especially as it was expounded by Augustine and Calvin. At the center of this theology stood a God who controlled all events according to His eternal arbitrary purpose. Every circumstance of life, however nonsensical from man's purview, was decreed by God. All that man needed to know about the divine will was revealed in the Bible, a book of law authoritative not only for the religious life but for the social and political order. His duty, as a follower of the law, was to promote its observance in society through exhortation and, if necessary, by force.

While Puritan thought pronounced the world to be good since it was a creation of God, it found man to be tragically depraved. This unfortunate state came about through the curse of original sin transmitted through Adam, the federal representative of the human race, and through man's innate desire to sin. Though weighed down with sinful propensities, man possessed faculties of reason and will which were free enough to render him responsible for his action. And yet God alone could perform the wonderful work of regeneration, bestowing grace upon whomsoever He chose for salvation. Such grace wrought a magical change in man's nature and empowered him to perform the works of righteousness.

The Puritan's meat was to be the willing servant of God. It was at once the sign of his election in the covenant of grace and the indication of his response to God's law. Since he had no way of knowing the divine plan for his life, he depended upon an analysis of his own thoughts and actions in order to judge his spiritual standing. Through a slavish keeping of diaries, the testimony of his conscience was recorded from year to year as if it might be of help in charting his spiritual progress. He stressed the place of good works and literally hurled himself into the task of building the Kingdom of God, which he saw to be society's chief purpose.

Since this world was continually a place of temptation, the Puritan had to be constantly on his guard, lest he be found cavorting with the "Divel." His only security lay in following a rigid pattern of personal conduct. The Puritan colonies, therefore, passed laws from time to time against mixed dancing, playing cards, shuffleboard or bowling, making minced pies, and celebrating Christmas. A Massachusetts law of 1653 made it illegal to clean house, cook, or even take a walk on Sunday. Nevertheless, many Puritans imbibed freely; taverns offered liquid refreshment, smoking, and dancing; and almost any bookseller kept a stock of playing cards. Election day, a popular occasion in New England, became as noted for its "spirits" as its spirituality.

Puritan zeal for learning was reflected in the early rise of educational institutions, founded primarily for the training of clergy. This was a necessary course of action since the Puritans, unlike the Anglicans, could not look to England for a steady recruitment of ministers. There was also a desire to transmit to the next generation the Renaissance spirit, which many of the New England intelligentsia had received at Cambridge. These interests bore fruit in the establishment (1636) of what became Harvard College, the first college in English America.

Despite its preoccupation with learning, the New England mind was gripped by a superstitious fear of the supernatural. This was an inheritance from old Europe, where popular belief in the occult led to witchcraft trials in which hundreds of persons were convicted and put to death. Witchcraft hysteria could be found in most of the American colonies, but only in New England were convicted witches executed. Between 1647 and 1663, fourteen victims were hanged in New England. The pestilence broke out again in 1688 and lasted until 1692; before it could be brought to an end, a score of persons and two dogs had been executed as witches.

As for the Indians, the average Puritan believed theoretically that the redeemed society which he was expected to build in the New World extended to his dark-skinned neighbors; in practice, he regarded them as objects to be pitied, more frequently despised. Some efforts, notably by

Thomas Mayhew, Jr., and John Eliot, were made to convert the natives, but the missionary endeavors met with relatively little success. Gradually the idea that the Indians belonged to an inferior and accursed race came to prevail, justifying their liquidation or enslavement by the colonists.

For many years the Puritans had taught that the church consists of those who give proof of their regeneration, together with their children. But many of these children upon attaining maturity failed to have a conversion experience and so made no public profession of their faith. In a sense, they were members of the church, yet it seemed questionable whether they could be admitted to the Lord's Supper. The problem became acute when this unconverted second generation presented their children for baptism. If these children were permitted to receive the sacrament and be considered church members upon reaching maturity, then the concept of the true church would have to be altered. If they were not considered members, then they could neither vote nor hold public office. In a colony where the voteless majority was becoming progressively larger, this was a matter of legitimate concern.

In 1657, the Ministerial Convention accepted a solution which provided that unregenerate members might transmit church membership and baptism to their children, but the latter could neither partake of the Lord's Supper nor participate in church elections. This compromise, known as the Half-Way Covenant, was finally approved by a synod of the churches in 1662.

The passage of the Half-Way Covenant was regarded by many as an invitation to further laxity. In certain areas church membership was granted to any individual who would promise to lead an ethical life. The result was that during the 1660's a decline in religious zeal was evidenced throughout New England. Soon the advisability of admitting half-way church members to the Lord's Supper was being discussed. In 1677, Solomon Stoddard, pastor of the church at Northampton, began to allow unconverted church members to partake of the sacrament because it might serve as a means by which they would become converted. After that time, the practice came to be known as Stoddardeanism. It came to be widely accepted in western Massachusetts. Spiritual vitality waned nonetheless, and the number of members in full communion with the church declined.

After 1660, the Puritan foundations were steadily weakened by pressures applied by the Crown. On demand by Charles II, the General Court passed a new law in 1665 which provided that all Englishmen who were freeholders, members of some community church, orthodox and of good character, and twenty-four years of age might request the court to be admitted to the full rights of citizens. The link between church and state was further weakened when, in 1684, the charter was revoked.

In the reorganization which followed the accession of William and Mary in 1689, Connecticut and Rhode Island resumed self-government under their old charters, while Massachusetts had to accept a royal governor with its new charter in 1691. All Christians, except Roman Catholics, were granted freedom of worship. Most distasteful to Puritans, however, was the provision which banned all religious tests for the suffrage. From that time, the church establishment was seriously weakened and rule by the saints was brought gradually to an end.

As the seventeenth century closed, it appeared to conservative leaders such as Increase Mather (1639-1723) that dangerous influences were abroad in the land. At Harvard, tutors were arguing that persons seeking reception as full communicant church members should not be required to make public testimony concerning their religious experience and that all baptized persons who contributed to a church should have a voice in the selection of its pastor. In order to neutralize the influence of Harvard, the development of a rival orthodox college was proposed. The result was the establishment of Yale College at New Haven. But, to the bitter disappointment of its founding fathers, the school soon proved to be as susceptible to liberalism as Harvard.

In certain other respects the conservatives in Connecticut were more successful. In 1708, an assembly of Congregational ministers and laymen convened at Saybrook and provided for the establishment of consociations in each county, with powers of oversight over local congregations; ministerial associations in each county, with responsibility for advising and examining ministerial candidates; and a general association, with undefined functions. This semi-Presbyterian "Saybrook Platform" won the approval of the Connecticut government, but was not made binding on all the churches. Gradually, the consociations took on more of the character of presbyteries; and Connecticut Puritans looked more to Middle Colony Presbyterians for fellowship than to their own denominational associates in Massachusetts, whose polity retained greater independence for the local churches.

Despite numerous appeals for reform, New England Puritanism manifested distinct signs of decay as the eighteenth century progressed. The relaxation of church standards brought no restoration of religious vitality; it simply confirmed the phlegmatic proclivities of a spiritually lethargic people. What was needed was a new crisis, a religious challenge which would capture the imagination and fire the soul. It would not be long in coming.

# CHAPTER FOUR

# Religious Diversity
# in the English Colonies

As the seventeenth century progressed, there appeared in the English colonies signs of that religious diversification which would become normative in American life. No orderly pattern marked its emergence. It was at once planned and spontaneous, immigrant and native born, concentrated and diffuse. Its single element of homogeneity lay in its vital principle—a passion for human rights.

## THE ROMAN CATHOLICS

Permanent Roman Catholic colonization in the English colonies was initiated in Maryland during the second quarter of the seventeenth century through the efforts of George Calvert, a Roman Catholic nobleman who was created Lord Baltimore in 1625. During the reign of Charles I, he received a grant of land north of Virginia; but before the charter could be issued, he died. Cecil Calvert (1606-1675), Lord Baltimore's eldest son, inherited the title and responsibilities of the proprietaryship. He was able to secure the financial support of many prominent Roman Catholics, but few of his coreligionists desired to settle in the new colony. Undoubtedly a minority of the first band of pilgrims were of the Roman Catholic faith. In guiding the preparations for the colony's founding, the second Lord Baltimore revealed both tact and good will. He directed his agents to maintain peace among the colonists and not permit any cause for offense, especially in matters pertaining to religion.

The first party of emigrants set sail from England in November 1633, and the following March disembarked at St. Clement's Island, where mass was celebrated. Through purchase from the Indians, the colonists acquired a large tract of land and established their first settlement at St. Mary's City.

Although the government of Maryland was controlled by Roman Catholics, all loyal English citizens who were Christians, according to the terms of the charter, were welcome. Lord Baltimore, in 1636, even required his governors to take an oath that they would show no favoritism to any individual for religious reasons. It has been charged that the Proprietor, in taking such action, was motivated by political considerations. To a certain extent that is probably true. Nevertheless, his utterances show him to be a man of great understanding and tolerance.

With the outbreak of the English Civil War in 1642, and the subsequent triumph of the parliamentary forces, Calvert feared that his charter would soon be revoked. In order to lessen that possibility, he endeavored to conciliate the ruling powers by urging the General Assembly to enact legislation which would insure freedom of worship for all Christians. The "Act Concerning Religion," passed in 1649, has frequently been heralded as one of the great advances in the history of religious freedom. Unquestionably it was liberal for its time, but it provided toleration for Christians alone. In its decree of death for persons who denied the deity of Jesus Christ or the Trinity, it provided less toleration than had been the practice throughout the colony. It thus represented a concession to the strict Puritan element then in control of the home government. Even this act was repealed in 1654, under the influence of the Puritan party, and Roman Catholics were denied the protection of the government and the exercise of their faith.

When Oliver Cromwell became Protector of England in 1653, Lord Baltimore sought and won his support. No sooner did the former regain proprietary control than religious toleration was restored to the colony. This arrangement prevailed during the reigns of Charles II and James II. After the revolution of 1688 and the succession of William and Mary, proprietary rule came to an end and Maryland became a royal colony. The General Assembly, convened by the new governor in 1692, abolished religious toleration for non-Trinitarians and Roman Catholics and passed the first legislation for the establishment of the Anglican Church.

At no time in the seventeenth century had Roman Catholicism in Maryland presented a serious threat to the Protestant majority. There were conversions from Protestantism, and Indians were won to the faith through the understanding of the Jesuit priests. But the gains could scarcely be called phenomenal. At the opening of the eighteenth century, Roman Catholics constituted less than ten per cent of the colony's population. Nevertheless, Anglican establishment brought with it increasing pressure on the Roman Catholic community. In 1704, the General Assembly made it illegal for a priest to say mass or to baptize any child whose parents were not Roman Catholic. In 1718, Roman Catholics were denied the franchise.

The intolerable conditions prompted many Roman Catholic families to seek haven in the newly founded colony of Pennsylvania, where they could enjoy freedom of worship. Before the outbreak of the Revolution, Roman Catholics could be found in every one of the thirteen colonies, though in extremely small numbers outside of Maryland and Pennsylvania.

Internal problems also harassed the Roman Catholic Church. The absence of a bishop in America created important administrative problems. It meant that the sacraments of confirmation and ordination, necessary to the ongoing life of the church, could not be conferred. The ordinances of religion were largely in the care of the Jesuit fathers, until the suppression of that order by the papacy in 1773. (The order was reinstated in 1814.) But never in the colonial period were there enough priests to minister to the growing Roman Catholic population. The result was that during the eighteenth century uncounted numbers of neglected Roman Catholic immigrants were permanently lost to the church. By the opening of the Revolution there were perhaps not more than 25,000 Roman Catholics in the colonies.

## THE BAPTISTS

The maelstrom which swept wave upon wave of Puritans out of England was responsible also for the exodus of other diverse religious elements in the population. None felt more sharply the sting of the Laudian persecution than that exceedingly protean group generally known as the Separatists. In early colonial America the Separatist cause was most vigorously represented by the scores of Baptist congregations which emerged along the Eastern seaboard. No uniform pattern marked their establishment. It was as if a whirlwind had plucked the seeds of Baptist dissent from the soil of England and carried them safely across the great ocean to a land ready for their cultivation. The first flowering was in New England.

The arrival of Roger Williams in orthodox Boston on February 5, 1631, set the stage for one of the most important experiments in American history—the founding of a colony on the principle of religious liberty. Born in London, Williams (c. 1603-1683) was reared in a family of middle-class Anglicans and educated at Cambridge. Though he accepted holy orders in the Church of England, his sympathies gradually became linked with Separatism.

By the time Williams arrived in New England, his Separatist inclinations were quite apparent. He refused to serve the congregation of the Boston Church because it held fellowship with the Anglican Church and recognized the jurisdiction of magistrates in matters of conscience. After a period of two years at Plymouth, where he labored with some success among the Narragansett Indians, he was called to assist the minister of the church at Salem. It was not long before trouble started. In a treatise written in 1633, the young theologian had been critical of King James' patents which conferred title to the lands of Massachusetts to the settlers. Since the land belonged to the Indians, how could James legally grant it to his subjects? The Puritans, through an ingenious method of allegory, had maintained that the Indians were an ungodly people who should be dispossessed of their territories by the new Israelites (the Puritans), whom God had led into the Promised Land. Williams insisted that the significance of the Israelite conquest of Palestine was spiritual and had no bearing on the present situation.

The critic was summarily ordered to appear before the General Court to give an accounting. This he did with great deference and, in apologetic humility, recanted and proffered his allegiance to the government. The matter was dropped, but only temporarily. Again Williams lashed out at the practices which seemed to him unjust, especially the interference of the civil power in religious matters. The General Court, in July 1635, charged him with "divers dangerous opinions" and the following October ordered him banished. When he continued to preach, officers were sent to put him on a ship bound for England. But a timely warning enabled him to escape into the frozen wilderness, later to find refuge in the region of Narragansett Bay.

After fourteen weeks of wandering, Williams stumbled upon the camp of the Narragansett Indians, who received him hospitably and cared for him throughout the winter. The following spring he and four other exiles founded a settlement at Seekonk, then moved on to the shore of Narragansett Bay where they founded Providence. This colony was to become a "shelter for those distressed in conscience."

In his insistence upon freedom of conscience, Williams championed a principle which was unique for his time. He argued that religious persecution involved the violation of conscience. A man might very well be mistaken in his views, but if sincere, he should not be molested. As for the relation of church and state, Williams advocated strict separation. Religion should never be used as a test of the fitness of a candidate for office nor should an elected official interfere in matters pertaining to conscience.

No sooner had Roger Williams established himself at Providence than he began to hold religious meetings in his home, preaching his doctrines of Separatism. Apparently he became impressed during this time by the teachings of certain Baptists who had arrived in the colony; their principles of adult conversion and believers' baptism seemed to him consistent with New Testament practice. In March 1639, Williams received baptism and then proceeded to baptize eleven other persons of like persuasion. The group, however, was not immersed, and there is no indication that this means was employed prior to 1649. Those who had been baptized organized a church, which some have claimed to be the first Baptist church in America. After a few months, Williams withdrew from the fellowship, preferring to be known henceforth simply as a "Seeker."

The Providence Church soon became embroiled in theological controversy. Some of the members who, like Williams, were Calvinists were challenged by an Arminian faction which held to free will. Finally, in 1652, the congregation divided into an Arminian group and a Calvinistic group which soon dissolved. Not until 1771 would a majority of the Providence congregation again adopt a Calvinistic confession.

Until the latter part of the seventeenth century the Baptist movement made slow progress outside of Rhode Island. In Massachusetts, President Henry Dunster of Harvard began to study the claims made for believers' baptism; by 1653, he felt compelled to speak out in public against the baptism of infants. Though he had won high respect and admiration for his brilliant achievements, his stand on baptism caused such a reaction that he was forced to resign from his post and was sentenced by the General Court to receive a public rebuke.

In 1665, the first Baptist church in Boston was organized in the home of Thomas Gould. Having been excommunicated from the Congregational Church, he and his followers were subjected to unusual trials in their new denominational connection, even to fines and imprisonment. But gradually the opposition lessened and, with the issuance of the new charter in 1691, persecution of Baptists virtually ended. Twenty-seven years later, Cotton Mather preached an ordination sermon at the Baptist Church in Boston. It was entitled "Good Men United."

The most promising center of Baptist growth was the Middle Colonies. Many Baptists were drawn to the Philadelphia area inasmuch as religious toleration was practiced in Pennsylvania and New Jersey. This development made advisable the formation of the Philadelphia Baptist Association, the first continuing Baptist association in America, in 1707. The association had great prestige and influence but no power as a

judicatory over its member churches. In 1742, the association adopted
as its doctrinal standard the London Confession of Particular Baptists of
1689. This denoted a decided trend among American Baptists toward
Calvinism and away from the once predominant Arminian persuasion.
A treatise on church discipline was also accepted; it was most urgently
needed, for as the association continued to grow, the churches required
instruction on their relation to it.

In the South, Baptist penetration was unimpressive prior to the Great
Awakening. Virginia made it clear from the beginning that dissenters
were unwelcome, especially Baptists. This apparently did not dissuade
a group of Arminian Baptists from settling in Isle of Wight County about
1700. Another group moved into northern Virginia between the years
1743 and 1756 and founded churches in Berkeley and Loudoun counties.
While some of these Baptists held to Arminianism, the majority accepted
a Calvinistic theology and were affiliated with the Philadelphia Association.

## THE FRIENDS

The introduction of Quakerism into the colonies was the result of a
concerted effort by its missionaries to win converts and replace Puritan
orthodoxy. Only after several decades would the movement derive its
strength largely through mass immigration. This accounts for the extreme diffuseness of the society and its unique effectiveness over a wide
area throughout the colonial period.

Before the arrival of the first Quaker missionaries in New England,
reports concerning their leader, George Fox, had filtered across the
Atlantic to Massachusetts and had placed the colony in a state of alarm.
When the missionaries, Ann Austin and Mary Fisher, arrived in Boston
in 1656, they were temporarily imprisoned and finally deported. Other
missionaries were similarly treated, but no sooner had one group been
deported than another arrived to take its place.

While Connecticut and New Haven, as well as New Netherland and
Virginia, passed laws against the Friends, no other colony enacted laws
as harsh as did Massachusetts. There four Quakers who refused to remain in exile were finally executed. A reaction set in and the law per-
mitting capital punishment for being a Friend was repealed, but the
Quakers suffered social discrimination for years to come. Of the New
England colonies, only Rhode Island allowed the Friends free exercise
of their religion.

The arrival of George Fox in the colonies in 1672 gave a considerable boost to the activities of the missionaries. Landing in Maryland in the spring of that year, he set out for Rhode Island where he remained two months, then started southward to Long Island and New Jersey, where he founded new meetings. His most important work was accomplished in the South, especially in North Carolina, Virginia, and Maryland.

With the emergence of New Jersey and Pennsylvania as Quaker centers, the prestige of the Society of Friends climbed with alacrity. During the 1670's, the rule of West Jersey became vested in a land company dominated by Friends and for the first time in their as yet brief history Friends were being charged with the responsibilities pertaining to government. When the province was opened to settlers, the proprietors announced that their purpose was to "lay a foundation for after ages to understand their liberty as men and Christians, that they may not be brought into bondage but by their own consent; for we put the power in the people."

Perhaps the most prominent among Quaker proprietors of the Jerseys was William Penn. Born in 1644, the son of a British admiral, Penn had been reared in the Anglican tradition, but in his manhood had been converted to Quakerism. In 1680, he petitioned the government for a grant of land, with the thought of establishing in America an asylum for the persecuted. That his request was granted the next year was due to the fact that Charles II was trying to satisfy an old indebtedness to Penn's father. Thus Penn became sole proprietor of the territory which was to be named Pennsylvania.

The enthusiasm Penn felt for his "Holy Experiment" was mirrored in the invitations which he extended to prospective colonists. He wanted them to know that in his judgment the role of government was "to support power in reverence with the people, and to secure the people from the abuse of power; for liberty without obedience is confusion, and obedience without liberty is slavery." The promise of freedom attracted the persecuted from the British Isles and from the Continent. At first the majority of the settlers were English and Welsh Quakers. Within a few years, however, immigrants would be coming in significant numbers from Germany, Holland, and France.

A study of Quaker life in Pennsylvania reveals an orientation which in some respects was not unlike the Puritan. Ascetic ideals and practices were as much a part of everyday life in Philadelphia as they were in Boston. Simplicity was the ideal in matters of fashion and interior decoration; idle pursuits such as dancing and attendance at the theater were thought to be unworthy of Christians and definitely not in the spirit of the New Testament Church. In other respects Quaker and Puritan ideals show a marked dissimilarity. While the Puritans esteemed an educated clergy and a theology which was intellectually appealing, the Friends preferred a ministry "called" though not trained and a simple pietistic faith which was emotionally satisfying.

From the standpoint of humanitarian principles, the Friends were far more advanced than their Puritan contemporaries. In Pennsylvania, punishment was less brutal than in New England, and prison conditions were superior to those in every other colony. Imprisonment of debtors was abolished by the personal action of Willian Penn. No other American settlement of the day could boast such an enlightened attitude toward its social problems.

One of the most outstanding of Penn's a hievements was his harmonious relationship with the Indians. He consistently treated them with fairness and justice, even fraternal affection. "I will consider you," he said to the Indians, "as the same flesh and blood with the Christians, and the same as if one man's body were to be divided into two parts."

The eighteenth century opened auspiciously for the community of Friends in the Quaker colonies. Many an enterprising Quaker became wealthy and influential and, believing his wealth to be a trust from God, administered it with frugality. Economic security, however, was all too often accompanied by an apparent absence of the spiritual fortitude which had typified the first settlers. Many who held positions of public trust maintained a formal allegiance to the Quaker movement, but their affiliation was due more to upbringing than to personal commitment. The situation grew worse after the London Yearly Meeting of 1737 declared that a man's family were to be considered members of the church if he held membership. And so the Friends followed in the steps of the Massachusetts Puritans, abandoning the necessary conversion experience in favor of membership by heredity. This road led downhill to an institutionalism that was both static and exclusive.

## The Presbyterians

American Presbyterianism was the child of English Puritanism and Scottish Presbyterianism, modified and reshaped in the colonial environment. In England, Puritanism had only gradually split into Presbyterian and Congregational wings; and in America, where the Congregational form was dominant, there were always tendencies toward Presbyterianism. During the latter half of the seventeenth century, Puritans from Connecticut planted churches on Long Island, in northern New Jersey, Pennsylvania, Maryland, Virginia, and South Carolina. Many invited Scottish Presbyterian ministers to preach to them, while at the same time they maintained their Congregational form of government. In some instances Presbyterian congregations called Congregational ministers into their service.

In theology, both Presbyterian and Congregational wings had been attracted to the Federal or Covenant system as enunciated in the Westminster Confession, prepared by English Puritans and Scottish Presbyterians in 1646. They differed chiefly in their doctrine of the church. In preference to a church which finds its reality in the local congregation, Presbyterians stressed the universal church, the congregation being merely a part of the body of Christ.

The major strength of colonial Presbyterianism was derived from the great migration of Scots from northern Ireland. Early in the seventeenth century, the English government tried to displace the Roman Catholic Irish population of northern Ireland by confiscating their property and inviting English and Scottish settlers to live there. It has been estimated that by 1641, an hundred thousand Scots had settled in Ulster; most of them were Presbyterians. Unusual difficulties, however, were destined to plague the newcomers. Their leases, originally modest, were soon doubled or trebled. Then came economic restrictions and the denial to Presbyterians of various political and ecclesiastical rights. By the early decades of the eighteenth century many of these harassed dissenters were turning their attention to the New World.

Beginning as a mere trickle in the late seventeenth century, the stream of immigration rose to full force after 1710, and the first sizable body of Presbyterians landed in Boston in 1718. Failing to receive an expected word of welcome, they moved on to the frontier. Disappointed but unperturbed by the reception in New England, Presbyterian immigrants turned more to the Middle Colonies and to the South. Many of the later settlers from Ulster did not sail to New England, but disembarked at the Delaware River towns of Philadelphia, Lewes, and New Castle. Another swarm of settlers poured into the Potomac Valley and traveled southwest into the Shenandoah. Charleston, South Carolina, became a leading port of entry after 1750.

Able leadership for the Presbyterian movement in the colonies was found in the person of Francis Makemie (1658-1708). Educated at the University of Glasgow, he was ordained in 1682 as a missionary to America. His early missionary labors took him over a wide area, notably along the coasts of Virginia and North Carolina and the eastern shore of Maryland. In 1692, he visited Philadelphia and inaugurated Presbyterian work there.

By the opening decade of the eighteenth century, Makemie saw the possibility of fostering unity among the widely scattered congregations through the creation of a presbytery. He summoned Presbyterian leaders to meet with him in Philadelphia and at this meeting, probably held in the spring of 1706, the first presbytery was organized. It was unique in that it was the earliest American judicatory to bind its churches into an intercolonial system for assistance and control. The presbytery had the advantage of being able to ordain and install its own clergy and regulate the affairs of congregations within its bounds without looking to some European ecclesiastical body for direction. It helped to instill a spirit of interdependence among its member organizations throughout the colonies and thus prepare the way for a strong national body after the severance of ties with Britain.

Neither questions of doctrinal uniformity nor matters of organization occupied the minds of the presbyters at the first meetings. No constitution was drawn up, and many details were left to be decided later. If the presbytery was patterned after any model, it was the Ulster form of presbytery. On the whole, however, the Presbyterian Church in America developed its own distinctive character and constituted an indigenous organization from its inception.

Like their Puritan counterparts, Presbyterians placed a high value on education, especially for the clergy. Candidates for the ministry were given rigorous training and were expected to show proficiency in the original languages of Scripture, theology, and the homiletic arts. Once ordained and installed as pastors, they conducted simple services which featured long scholarly expositions of Scripture. Their congregations accustomed themselves to protracted services of worship, at the conclusion of which they would repair to the local tavern for rest and refreshment, returning to the church in time for the afternoon service.

By 1716, forty churches and 3,000 communicant members were affiliated with the presbytery. To Presbyterian leaders the time seemed right to divide the judicatory into four presbyteries and unite them into a body to be known as the Synod. The original presbytery, therefore, decreed in 1716 that the presbyteries of Philadelphia, New Castle, Long Island, and Snow Hill should be constituted; only the first three materialized. The powers of the new Synod, which met for the first time in 1717, were rather vague. Having been given no constitutional authority, it served as a kind of presbytery exercising general jurisdiction over three regional courts.

The opening decades of the eighteenth century witnessed a widening rift among Presbyterians in Britain and America over questions of theology and discipline. In Scotland and Ireland the courts of the church had combated the rising tides of Deism and Arminianism by forcing subscription to the Westminster Confession as a prerequisite to ordination. This decision served only to inspire widespread indignation. By the 1720's, tension in the Scottish and Irish judicatories had become explosive.

In America, the Scotch-Irish element found increasing dissatisfaction with the Puritan party, which opposed any compulsory subscription to creeds, confessions, or articles of church polity. When an overture, which provided that ministers and licentiates must subscribe strictly to the Westminster Confession and Catechisms, was introduced in Synod in 1727, a vigorous debate ensued. The Synod reached no decision; but when the measure was brought up again in 1729, Jonathan Dickinson, pastor of the church at Elizabethtown, New Jersey, led the liberal party in opposing it. As he saw it, a creed was only a systematic statement of the general beliefs of a given denomination and one of many guides available for the study of the Bible. When its purpose went beyond leading men to the Bible, there would be contention and strife within the Christian fellowship; the function of religion would be reduced to the formulation of rational truths about God.

An Adopting Act was passed in 1729, but it was a compromise measure and only in this way received unanimous approval. It provided that ministers of the Synod accept the "essential and necessary articles" of the Presbyterian standards. Since the Synod did not determine which articles were necessary, the matter could be left largely to the presbyteries. But the conflict between various warring elements in the church had not been fully extinguished. It lingered as a smoldering fire which would again burst into full flame amid the tensions of the Great Awakening.

## THE GERMAN BODIES

Despite the tremendous spiritual energy which Martin Luther had infused into German Protestantism, the century following his death witnessed the steady ebb of the Protestant tide. The Lutheran establishment, being concerned largely with an intellectual formulation of scriptural truth, came to interpret saving faith in terms of intellectual assent. Strict orthodoxy became the *sine qua non* of religion, a condition which led to heresy trials, almost constant struggles with other Christian bodies, and the demoralization of the country's religious and moral life. No less important was the devastating Thirty Years' War, which left Germany impoverished.

Signs of religious revival appeared in the mid-seventeenth century with the nascence of Pietism. It stood for mystical experience, practical and intense preaching, the priesthood of all believers, and piety and moderation in conduct. While the movement centered in the Lutheran Church, it affected all branches of German Protestantism. None entered more completely into its spirit than the various sectaries which stemmed from the left wing of the Reformation. When, in the final quarter of the seventeenth century, the invasions of the Palatinate by Louis XIV forced the Germans to flee their homes, many settled in the American colonies.

The first German settlement was begun in 1683 at Germantown, near Philadelphia, by refugees from the Palatinate. They were members of the Mennonite sect, which stood in the main stream of the Anabaptist movement. The sect took its name from the Dutch Anabaptist, Menno Simons (1492-1559). A second group of German-speaking Swiss Mennonites arrived about 1710 and settled in what is now Lancaster County. Some of these settlers belonged to a conservative sect known as the Amish, which found its origins in a seventeenth-century schism among the Mennonites. They became known for doctrinal rigidity and plain dress, especially the wearing of hooks and eyes in preference to buttons, which they considered vain.

Perhaps the most remarkable of the German sectaries was the Moravian Brethren or Unitas Fratrum, which grew out of the evangelical movement in Bohemia inspired by John Huss in the fifteenth century. In 1722, a little band of Moravians made arrangements with a Saxon nobleman, Nicolaus Ludwig, Count von Zinzendorf (1700-1760), to settle on his estate at Herrnhut. Zinzendorf, a Lutheran with pietistic inclinations, soon began participating in the activities of the Moravian Church and finally emerged as its bishop. Herrnhut then became the nucleus of a vast missionary enterprise which reached into other lands.

Upon hearing the news that a colony had been founded in Georgia by James Oglethorpe, Zinzendorf sought and gained his approval for the admission of Moravian missionaries. From 1735 to 1740, a group of Moravians, under the leadership of Augustus Spangenberg, conducted evangelistic work among the Indians and Negro slaves in the vicinity of Savannah. They then settled in Pennsylvania, first at Nazareth and later at Bethlehem. From this center they launched a wide-scale campaign to win converts to their Christocentric doctrine which emphasized the vicarious atonement. Possibly their most successful missionary work among the Indians of western Pennsylvania and Ohio was begun in 1765 by David Zeisberger. A remarkable degree of civilization was achieved and numerous bands of Indians were won to Christianity.

The unfortunate circumstances which prompted the German sectaries to flee from the homeland to America were similarly evident in the decision of many Lutherans and Reformed to emigrate. The latter groups, however, being accustomed to a close church-state relationship and a non-congregational polity, maintained full connections with European ecclesiastical bodies throughout the colonial period. From a numerical standpoint, the Lutherans were the most important German religious group to settle in America. The deluge began shortly after the opening of the eighteenth century. Dwelling first in such places as Falckner's Swamp (New Hanover), Germantown, and Philadelphia, the immigrants gradually pushed into the interior, crossing the Susquehanna and moving southward in Maryland and Virginia.

Most of the early Lutheran settlers had been influenced by pietism and had come to regard the Christian life as one of devotion and love. They cherished not only their Bible and catechism but devotional classics such as Johann Arndt's *True Christianity*. Preaching and the sacraments were a great source of consolation. Unfortunately, ministerial service was seldom available in the colonies. The Swedish and Finnish Lutheran churches were always ready to help; yet, without a steady supply of clergy, it was quite natural that some should change over to other religious bodies or simply allow their spiritual life to remain unnurtured. Besides, in their destitute condition, few congregations were financially able to support a pastor.

A new era in colonial Lutheran history began with the arrival of Henry Melchior Muhlenberg (1711-1787) in 1742. With indefatigable zeal this German minister threw himself into the work of reformation. He assumed the pastoral oversight of the Germantown congregation and founded a school for each local church. Gradually he extended his influence over other areas and new congregations were organized. His *Halle Reports* were published in Germany, where they captured the public imagination and, as a result, won both men and money for the cause.

Undoubtedly, Muhlenberg's most important contribution to American Lutheranism was his forming of a synod in 1748 for the purpose of achieving increased cooperation among pastors and churches. Then known as the "United Pastors," the synod is now denominated the Ministerium of Pennsylvania. Its first act was to adopt a uniform liturgy suggested by Muhlenberg and two other pastors.

From 1755 to 1759, there were no meetings of the synod. It was a time of discouragement, with almost constant friction between the "United Pastors" and the European leaders who could not quite appreciate the needs of the American church. The arrival of Charles Magnus Wrangel in 1759 as provost of the Swedish churches was thus heralded, even among the Germans, as a sign of better things to come. Wrangel and Muhlenberg became fast friends, and the sound counsel which the latter received from the learned Swedish leader explains in large measure Muhlenberg's decision to revive the synod in 1760. Thenceforth, the synod, with improved organization, exerted a powerful influence over the major proportion of American Lutherans and proved to be an important asset in the development of the church.

The same forces which prompted German Lutherans to settle in the colonies were responsible for the arrival of their Reformed compatriots. The guiding spirit of the Reformed Church in America was John Philip Boehm, a schoolteacher from Worms who settled in Montgomery County, Pennsylvania, in 1720. Widely recognized for his piety, he was persuaded to conduct informal religious services among the pastorless people and finally to accept clerical responsibilities, though he was not then ordained. In 1729, he was ordained to the ministry by the Classis of Amsterdam.

What Muhlenberg was to the Lutherans, Michael Schlatter (1716-1790) was to the Reformed. A native of St. Gall, Switzerland, he taught for some years in Holland, where he was ordained. In 1746, the Synods of Holland, having agreed to assume responsibility for the German Reformed congregations in America, appointed Schlatter to visit the scattered churches and to establish an ecclesiastical organization as soon as possible. At once he began a tour of the settlements and endeavored to infuse new life into the congregations. In October, 1746, he met with several of his fellow clergy in Philadelphia for the purpose of laying the groundwork for the establishment of a synod or Coetus; the following September the Coetus met for the first time in that same city. This body, however, remained under the general supervision of the Classis of Amsterdam until after the Revolution.

# CHAPTER FIVE

# The Great Awakening

To many thoughtful observers living in the colonies during the opening decades of the eighteenth century, it was apparent that the wellsprings of religious fervor in America were rapidly drying up. Where once there was ardent devotion to the things of the spirit now there were self-satisfaction and lethargic indifference. Multitudinous forces contributed to this unhappy condition. The development of commerce in the colonies helped to focus attention on materialistic interests. Conflicts with the English government over its efforts to abolish representative government turned the thoughts of the colonists to politics. Yet the problem cannot be dismissed as purely extraecclesiastical. Fervor and zeal were all too often missing from the churches; religion was confined to a vague discontent over sin in general and enthusiasm in particular.

## THE MIDDLE-COLONY REVIVAL

The spark which kindled the flames of reawakened piety was ignited by a Dutch Reformed minister, Theodore J. Frelinghuysen (1691-1747). A German educated in the Calvinist tradition, he was ordained in 1717 and three years later began a powerful ministry to several Dutch congregations in New Jersey. This ministry was supported by evangelistic preaching, regular pastoral visitation, and the maintenance of strict discipline. Frelinghuysen's labors in the Raritan River valley soon bore fruit in manifold conversions; and, in spite of opposition from those who objected to his somewhat unconventional methods, the revival spread like wildfire into other Dutch communities.

A noteworthy impetus to the revival among the Presbyterians was given by William Tennent, who moved to Neshaminy, Pennsylvania, in 1727, and founded a "Log College" for training a ministry, and Gilbert Tennent, his son, who pastored the Presbyterian church at New Brunswick, New Jersey. Gilbert Tennent saw the root of the religious problem to be the "presumptuous Security" of his people and their false identification of sound doctrine with saving faith. He felt called to illumine their self-satisfied lives and inspire them to an inner conviction that must necessarily express itself in gracious works. His flaming oratory evoked from his parishioners violent reactions; sobs, shrieks, and groans emitted from the house of worship as members gave vent to their emotions. Other congregations soon caught the spirit of the revival and passed it on to hundreds of noncommunicants who identified themselves with the Christian fellowship. By 1738, it was necessary to organize another judicatory, the Presbytery of New Brunswick.

One of the most influential contributors to the revival was the Anglican evangelist, George Whitefield (1714-1770). Educated at Oxford, where he had been an associate of John Wesley, he was ordained in 1736. Two years later he spent a few months in Georgia, where he not only won popularity as a preacher but also as a humanitarian whose chief passion was to found an orphan house. After returning to England, he preached to thousands of persons at great outdoor services. By 1739, he was back in America. At Philadelphia there was such demand to hear him preach that he had to speak from the gallery of the Court House to nearly 6,000 people standing in the streets. Benjamin Franklin was deeply impressed by his reasonable preaching and complimented him publicly.

From the outset, Presbyterians had viewed the revival with mixed feelings. The Scotch-Irish party, strong for subscription, had looked with jaundiced eyes upon the revivalists, especially upon the revivalist-controlled Presbytery of New Brunswick. In order to frustrate their efforts, the opponents of the revival presented to Synod an overture requiring candidates for ordination who had not graduated from a New England or European college to take an examination before a committee of Synod; the overture was passed. When the Presbytery of New Brunswick, in clear violation of the directive, proceeded to ordain a graduate of the "Log College," the Synod, in 1741, dominated by the Scotch-Irish faction, expelled the recalcitrant judicatory. In 1745, this presbytery, joined by the presbyteries of New York and New Castle, organized the Synod of New York, which came to be known as the "New Side." During the thirteen years of its independent existence, this Synod, strengthened by the dynamic Christocentric preaching of the revivalists, made notable gains in the Middle Colonies and the South. The conservative "Old Side" Synod of Philadelphia, weakened by a high percentage of mediocre and lethargic clergy, entered a period of decline.

Eventually both sides grew tired of the schism. A Plan of Union was presented and adopted by both synods in 1758, bringing to an end the unfortunate estrangement. It provided that ministers should subscribe to the Confession and give greater deference to the authority of church judicatories. It also provided that ministerial candidates should be examined as to their "experimental acquaintance with religion." Obviously neither side had gained a significant victory.

## THE EDWARDEAN AWAKENING

The forces which initiated the revival in the Middle Colonies were also at work in the New England Awakening, which was inaugurated by Jonathan Edwards (1703-1758). Born at East Windsor, Connecticut, the son and grandson of Congregational ministers, he was educated at Yale. After holding a brief Presbyterian pastorate, he returned to Yale as tutor. In 1727, he became assistant minister of the Congregational church at Northampton, Massachusetts, which was pastored by his grandfather, Solomon Stoddard.

Edwards found the local citizenry to be "very insensible of the things of religion," having lapsed into the degeneracy of the times. This situation he blamed partially upon the growing trend toward Arminianism, with its doctrine of general atonement and high view of man. What was needed was something to convict men of their sin and shock them out of their complacency. Thus, in preaching he came to stress man's complete dependence on God. But unlike Calvin, who centered his theology on the sovereignty of God, Edwards based his upon the unworthiness of man.

As early as 1733, it was noticed that young people were coming more regularly to church and were giving greater heed to the admonitions of their minister. By 1734, a sense of anxiety, born of the fear of God's wrath, had gripped the townspeople; within six months, 300 persons had been converted and received into the church. The spirit of the revival soon spread into other communities such as South Hadley, Suffield, Green River, Hatfield, and Enfield. In Windsor and East Windsor, Connecticut, there was a general awakening. Thus the revival diffused itself through the Connecticut Valley and continued to do so through successive years.

A powerful impetus to the revival was given by George Whitefield, who arrived in New England in 1740. At his first meeting in Boston, he states that he preached to 4,000 persons and on the following Sunday to 15,000. With the exception of Charles Chauncy of First Church, who opposed him in every way, he received the support of the city's leading ministers. While Edwards was formal and reserved, Whitefield was emotional and sensational. Both preached the love of God, but Edwards placed more stress on God's wrath while Whitefield emphasized man's hope. Their most emphatic agreement was on the supernatural nature of conversion and the necessity of a conversion experience. The core of their religious thought was the doctrine of salvation.

Jonathan Edwards was more than the leader of a revival; he was a philosopher and theologian in his own right. He was never satisfied with a moralistic conception of piety. Religion to him was not so much morality as an experience of the reality of God, a feeling of divine joy and happiness. On the other hand, he looked upon God as a sovereign ruler who, in His wrath, holds the unconverted sinner over the pit of hell. Thus in Edwards' thought we find a combination of the immanent God who illumines the heart of man, and the transcendent God who strikes down the sinner.

One of Edwards' most important contributions to American theology was his idea of virtue and the Christian life. It is difficult to comprehend unless one understands that for him the universe is an emanation from God and that it possesses reality only to the extent that it partakes of the divine nature. God, being infinite, has the most being and is therefore the most excellent; other beings are excellent to the extent that they possess existence. Virtue is good will and love for being, which in its fullness is God. The love which one holds for other beings ought to depend upon the degree to which they possess existence or partake of God's being.

It might seem that this concept would be destructive of evangelism, inasmuch as love would be involved in preaching to sinners, many of whom could be expected to be among the nonelect. But Edwards would have rejected this philosophy. He justified missions not as a means of showing one's love for the unconverted but as a willing response to God's revealed will. This idea had important implications for the nineteenth-century Protestant attitude toward missions.

What was unique about the Great Awakening was that it touched every area of life. Urban dweller, rural settler, rich man, poor man, savant, illiterate—all felt the force of its power. Beginning as a frontier phenomenon, it gradually spread into the cities where it was advanced by both great and obscure. By 1741 and 1742, the revival had reached the peak of its influence. Everywhere there were evidences of concern and repentance. Young people especially seemed eager to participate in personal evangelism. The effect was to increase the sectarian ideal in the churches which based church membership on a voluntary act of commitment. This would help to widen the gap between church and state and prepare Congregationalism for the acceptance of separatism in the period following independence.

But if there was strength in the revival, there was also weakness. As it progressed, certain evangelists began to resort to sensational and sometimes offensive practices which cast embarrassment and reproach upon the movement. Shortly after Whitefield's departure, the tempestuous Gilbert Tennent blew into New England to fan the flames of enthusiasm. But his flamboyant mannerisms and his raucous rantings on hellfire and damnation themes gradually evoked the criticism of more sensitive spirits, who contributed mightily to his disparagement. By this time New England Congregationalists had virtually split into two camps. On one side were the "New Lights" or protagonists of the revival headed by Edwards; on the other were the "Old Lights" led by Charles Chauncy. Feeling over the issue frequently ran so high that congregations split asunder.

At Northampton, the congregation was becoming increasingly dissatisfied with its minister; by 1748, there was open division between Edwards and his people. With his dismissal as pastor two years later, a ministry of more than twenty years was ignominiously brought to an end. For a few years Edwards ministered to some English families and undertook missionary work among the Indians at Stockbridge; then, in 1757, he was called as president of the College of New Jersey, a young institution which had shown sympathy for the revival. Some months later he fell victim to smallpox and died in his fifty-fifth year. His passing symbolized the end of the New England Awakening. The decades just ahead would witness a resurgence of rationalism, spiritual lethargy, theological controversy, and political upheaval.

## The Baptist and Methodist Phases

New England Baptists were slow to become involved in the Great Awakening largely because prior to the revival most of their congregations followed Arminianism, and an evangelistic campaign rooted in Calvinistic theology was not to their liking. The practice of infant baptism among the revivalists also contributed to Baptist aloofness. Nevertheless, some Baptists, voicing opposition to Arminianism and cold formalism, withdrew from their congregations and founded new churches. In many cases Congregationalist laymen in churches where there was opposition to the revival established "Separate" congregations only to affiliate later with the Baptist movement. These newcomers to the Baptist fold did much to further the doctrines of Calvinism within the denomination.

The Middle-Colony Baptists also felt the influence of the revival. In the Philadelphia Association, which leaned heavily toward Calvinism, there was a notable intensification of evangelistic efforts. However, the chief gains in membership were made on the southern frontier. There Baptist ministers, for the most part lacking in formal education, were able to establish a remarkable rapport with rude frontiersmen who could neither read nor write. They preached with persuasive zeal a simplified Gospel which struck deeply into the heart of the hearer and called forth a verdict. If many were won to the church in a moment of frenzied excitement brought on by a bombastic revivalist who had taken little time to instruct them in the obligations of their profession, it was to be expected. Under the circumstances, emotion was a more effective instrument than reason.

As the first great colonial awakening drew to its close, Methodism was introduced to America. While it had originated within the Anglican Church, it had departed radically from Anglican thought in emphases. Its stress was upon conversion instead of baptism, upon personal religious experience rather than formal communicant membership in a church institution.

Its founder, John Wesley (1703-1791), was an Anglican clergyman who, after a mystical religious experience in 1738, pledged his life to the cause of evangelism. As he saw salvation, it was not merely a gift of the Holy Spirit at conversion; it was the Christian life itself, a continuing escape from sin and the unceasing attainment of holiness. One of the best ways one could give evidence of his conversion would be to renounce the usual pleasures of society, such as card playing, dancing, gambling, and attendance at the theater. The influence which this idea would have upon evangelical Protestant conceptions of morality throughout the nineteenth century in England and America would be prodigious.

In 1769, two English local preachers, John King and Robert Williams, reached America. King introduced Methodism into Baltimore, while Williams carried on an itinerant ministry in southern Virginia, where a revival was already in progress under the leadership of Devereux Jarratt, an Anglican clergyman. Williams received considerable support from Jarratt, a fact which helps to account for the rapid growth of the Methodist societies in the South.

Meanwhile, Wesley commissioned Richard Boardman and Joseph Pilmoor to serve as official representatives in the Middle Colonies. Landing in October, 1769, Boardman took over the work in Now York, while Pilmoor served for a time in Philadelphia and then went on an extensive missionary tour through the Middle Colonies and the South. The most important appointee, in 1771, was Francis Asbury (1745-1816); within a decade he would emerge as the guiding genius of the denomination

## The Aftermath of the Revival

The full impact of the Great Awakening upon American life can scarcely be appreciated through a study limited to religious institutions, important though they be. Clearly, the revival established an evangelistic pattern which would be followed again and again on the frontier and even in the cities. It helped to mold a theology for the American environment and to transform immigrant denominations into indigenous bodies. But it did much more. It fostered a progressive democratization of religion by diminishing sectarian insularity and strengthening the ideal of one common humanity. Politically, it proved indirectly to be of assistance to those groups, notably in the South, which were opposed to establishments. More significantly, it served to tie the colonies together in a new way. The names of Edwards, Tennent, and Whitefield became symbols of a growing interdependence in the colonies and a wider sense of community. In short, the revival helped to break down localism and thus support those forces which would give rise to a new nation.

The Great Awakening figured just as prominently in the upsurge of a new humanitarian impulse. In every section of the country there were evidences of a deeper concern for man, a wider commitment to his amelioration. The idealism of the times found expression in sundry causes dedicated to the spiritual, intellectual, or physical advancement of Indians, Negro slaves, orphans, college students, and other favored persons. In some cases these movements stemmed directly from the revival effort in America; in others they traced their origins to pietistic or humanitarian strains planted within the denomination in its embryonic stage. There were instances in which they were promoted by liberal or secular forces which were somehow caught up and swept along in the fast-moving currents of reform. It is ironic that the humanitarianism of the Awakening, God-centered as it was, should have contributed to the rise of doctrines which emphasized man and his good works. But it was inevitable. The restless, optimistic spirit of the frontier channeled the course of American thought in that direction.

In New England, Jonathan Edwards was followed by a group of disciples who labored to refute Arminianism but who undermined the Calvinistic emphasis upon God and shifted it to man. Most important was Samuel Hopkins (1721-1803). At the center of his system was the love, rather than the justice, of God. He believed that man has freedom and that salvation is through his volition. In the process of salvation, God performs the work of regeneration to which man responds in the act of conversion, which takes place instantaneously. The death of Christ as an act of Atonement is not limited to the elect, as in Calvinism, but is for all men. Those who respond through conversion manifest their new state in works of holiness which grow out of "disinterested benevolence," or concern for the greatest good of all. Such persons will be willing to accept even the detrimental effects of evil in order to preserve others from greater evil or to achieve some worthy end.

Meanwhile, a decidedly more liberal position was developing in sharp contrast to the theology of Edwards and his successors. Its roots may be traced to the English Presbyterian theologian, John Taylor (1694-1761), who rejected the doctrine of original sin and maintained that since guilt is personal it cannot be transferred from one person to another. Each person is born with the capacity to be righteous or sinful. This view caught hold in the Boston area where a reaction was building up to the revival and its Calvinistic concepts. The chief representatives of Taylorism in New England were Samuel Webster and Charles Chauncy.

While the churches were embroiled in theological polemic, a powerful philosophical force was steadily gaining strength. Since the seventeenth century, Deism, which stood for greater distrust of the supernatural in religion, greater faith in the sufficiency of man's reason, and greater trust in man's moral ability to live the good life, had been making a considerable impact upon English intellectual life. It gradually spread to the colonies, gaining steady momentum throughout the eighteenth century.

Doctrines which stressed God's activity through nature and man's innate goodness had a certain natural appeal to the American mind; to certain groups of intellectuals and anti-revivalists they were highly gratifying. In the place of "enthusiasm" they could substitute reason; in the place of faith, good works. Many Deists maintained a nominal connection with the church without adhering to its doctrines, as in the case of George Washington. Others, such as Jefferson and Franklin, exhibited an attitude of friendliness toward organized religion without becoming communicants of any church.

At its best, Deism was a champion of spiritual and intellectual liberation. Its power, like that of the Great Awakening, lay in its catholicity. Its passion was man and his betterment. If it was naïve in its estimate of mankind, at least it erred in a positive direction. It envisioned an ideal society, ruled by reason, ennobled by benevolence, and blessed by freedom. There can be no doubt but that it played a profound role in the making of the revolutionary generation.

# CHAPTER SIX

# Religion
# and the Birth of a Nation

## THE CHURCHES AND THE REVOLUTION

Except for the Great Awakening, no forces of consequence had acted prior to the Revolution to break down the social, economic, and religious walls which divided the American colonies. Indeed, there seemed to be a profound horror of consolidation. So regnant was this feeling that the colonists, many of them loyal members of the Church of England, labored to prevent the introduction of the Anglican episcopate into America lest it begin a process of setting up a complete autocratic hierarchy with centralized authority.

Nevertheless, certain intellectual factors helped to prepare the way for revolution and to bind the people, out of necessity, into a confederation. Among these were: the idea of fundamental law and the natural rights of the individual as guaranteed by that law; the "social contract" idea that government is created by consent of the people; and the idea, taught by Calvin, that when there is oppression, the representatives of the people have the right to resist.

Three religious factors, in particular, had an important and direct bearing on the Revolution. The first was the Great Awakening. In this great revival, the American colonists discovered for the first time a common emotional and intellectual challenge. Intercolonial leaders such as Edwards, Whitefield, and Tennent did much to foster cooperation and union among various religious groups and to lessen racial and denominational tensions. This emphasis, together with an increasing shift of population throughout the colonies, fostered a spirit of community. By drawing many nominal adherents of the Anglican Church into the fellowship of the evangelical denominations the revival weakened the chain which bound the colonies to England.

A second contributing factor was fear of Anglican ecclesiasticism by evangelicals. Since colonial Anglicanism was hindered by its inability to administer confirmation and ordination in America, it was natural that from time to time some of its leaders would agitate for the establishment of an episcopate which would make these functions possible. The sending of a bishop to America might actually have been a step toward independence, for it would have whetted the American appetite for self-rule. But evangelical leaders, especially Congregationalist and Presbyterian, strongly objected to this attempt on the ground that it was another cause for interference from the British government.

A third factor was concern over the Quebec Act of 1774. In 1763, England, upon receiving the French dominions in Canada as part of the settlement which terminated the Seven Years' War, agreed to extend toleration to Roman Catholics. But eleven years later, when Britain included the Northwest Territory, a triangular area between the Ohio and Mississippi Rivers, within the boundaries of the Province of Quebec, a storm of protest was raised. It seemed to many Protestants that Roman Catholic influence would be coming too close to New England and the Middle Colonies for comfort.

During the pre-revolutionary era, the pulpit was the most important single force in the colonies for shaping and controlling public opinion. The minister was usually the best-educated person in the community, and his words were regarded as having considerable authority behind them, even when they dealt with political philosophy. When fired with zeal to preach independence and resistance to royal authority, he could exercise a tremendous influence over his congregation. In light of the fact that Congregationalist, Presbyterian, Dutch Reformed, and Baptist ministers were almost overwhelmingly on the side of the Revolution and that they were supported to a large extent by the Lutherans and German Reformed, one can understand the importance of the role played by the clergy in this tumultuous era.

Edmund Burke, who understood the colonies as well as any Englishman, reported to Parliament that the Americans were largely Protestant dissenters from the Church of England. They had grown accustomed to the freest discussion of all religious questions, and this had brought about extreme individualism. The right of private judgment, which they reserved for themselves in spiritual matters, and the right to elect and dismiss religious leaders had been carried over into politics, a fact which accounted for their pronounced liberalism. But perhaps the most important factor in American patriotism was the conviction that from the outset God had guided their adventure in the new land. Fortified by a dream and a destiny, they could not be overwhelmed.

Of the four leading denominations in the colonies at the opening of the Revolution, three gave extraordinary support to the patriot cause. No religious body surpassed the Congregationalists in contributions to the revolutionary effort. The entire force of New England was thrown into the struggle, and this force was started and controlled largely by the clergy. One Loyalist from New York wrote to a friend in London that the New England ministers were wicked, malicious, and inflammatory; their pulpits were "converted into Gutters of Sedition," and they substituted politics for the Gospel.

It has been asserted that the "sturdy Republicanism" of the Presbyterians gave them "an influence over the course of the Revolution out of all proportion to their numbers." Joseph Galloway, a Pennsylvania Tory, said that the foes of the English government in 1774 were "Congregationalists, Presbyterians and smugglers." Concerning the composition of the Continental army he reported that one-fourth were natives of America, one-half were Irish, and the other fourth were English and Scottish. A considerable number of Presbyterians were leaders of the Revolution. Many were graduates of the College of New Jersey where they had first been exposed to the principles of freedom of conscience and government by the consent of the governed. Nine of the college's alumni became members of the Federal Constitutional Convention in 1787, and its president, John Witherspoon (1723-1794), a Scottish immigrant, was the only clergyman to sign the Declaration of Independence.

Baptist congregations gave intense support to the movement for independence. Persecuted as they were under English law, they could not help but favor a cause which permitted them full liberty of conscience. They generally aided the Revolution because they hoped for fairer treatment under the new government and because ideologically their democratic polity and compact theory of government harmonized more nearly with the principles which ruled the patriot side.

The Anglican Church was, of the major denominations, most loyal to the English King. Yet out of its ranks came many of the most outspoken patriots, men who would give their lives for freedom from the tyranny of that same ruler. It is significant that two-thirds of the signers of the Declaration of Independence were affiliated with the Anglican Church. In general, however, Anglican laymen were very much divided in their allegiance. In the South and the Middle Colonies the majority were patriotic, while in New England they tended to side with the British. In the South most Whigs belonged to the Church of England; in New England no outstanding Whig was an Anglican. As for the clergy, a majority in Virginia were Loyalist, though a substantial minority, perhaps one-third, were hostile to the crown. In the northern colonies, especially Massachusetts, Connecticut, and New York, the clergy were even more inclined toward loyalty to England than in the South.

## RELIGION AND THE NEW POLITICAL ORDER

Before the ink could dry on the Declaration of Independence, agitation had arisen in certain colonies to bring to an end the favors enjoyed by established churches. In Virginia, where more than half of the population was identified with dissenting bodies, a tidal wave of indignation threatened to engulf the Anglican establishment; much of its force came from Baptists and Presbyterians. In June 1776, the House of Burgesses adopted a Declaration of Rights which provided complete religious freedom but did not abolish the establishment. The following December, the first republican legislature of Virginia, the General Assembly, passed an act which made it incumbent for no man to attend or support in any fashion a church not of his choice. Thomas Jefferson regarded the legislation highly significant since for all practical purposes it spelled the doom of the establishment. Finally, in 1785, the Assembly adopted Jefferson's Bill for Establishing Religious Freedom, which provided that men shall be "free to profess . . . their opinions in matters of religion, and that the same shall in no wise diminish, enlarge, or effect their civil capacities." Other southern states soon followed the lead of Virginia and terminated official connections with the Anglican Church. In New York, the only state north of the Mason and Dixon line where anything an Anglican establishment had prevailed, the connection between church and state was severed by the constitution of 1777.

The situation in New England, where Congregationalism was established, was far different. Since the establishments there had been overwhelmingly on the side of independence, the severance of political ties with England had little bearing on their future status. Naturally the clerical leaders and prominent laymen of Congregationalism were anxious to preserve the *status quo* and exerted what influence they had, which was considerable, to maintain the establishment.

After the turn of the century, a concerted effort to bring the establishment in Connecticut to an end was begun by Baptists, Methodists, Unitarians, Universalists, Friends, and most Episcopalians. These were allied with the Republican Party in opposition to the Federalists, who were supported by the Congregationalists. By 1817, the Republicans had amassed enough strength to win at the polls and introduce a more liberal influence in the state government. The following year, 1818, a constitutional convention, assembled at Hartford, drew up a constitution which stipulated that "no preference shall be given by law to any Christian sect or mode of worship." Lyman Beecher, the eminent Congregationalist minister, has recorded his impressions on that fateful day which brought disestablishment.

> It was as dark a day as ever I saw. The odium thrown upon the ministry was inconceivable. The injury done to the cause of Christ, as we then supposed, was irreparable. For several days I suffered what no tongue can tell *for the best thing that ever happened to the State of Connecticut.* It cut the churches loose from dependence on state support. It threw them wholly on their own resources and on God.[1]

In New Hampshire the struggle over the question of establishment was somewhat less bitter. The first state to adopt a constitution (January 5, 1776), it included no provision concerning religion; Congregationalism, however, remained the established faith. During the ensuing years, mounting antagonism toward the maintenance of an establishment, spurred on by the Baptists, led to the enactment of more liberal policies. Finally, in 1817, the legislature placed all churches in the state on essentially the same legal basis, bringing to an end the Congregational establishment.

Despite strong liberal forces which were operative in Massachusetts during the revolutionary era, the Bay State was the tardiest in achieving disestablishment. Its first constitution, adopted in 1780, contained a Declaration of Rights which recognized the right of every man to worship God according to the dictates of his own conscience; it also authorized the government to make provision "for the support and maintenance of public Protestant teachers of piety, religion, and morality." Dissenters, however, might earmark their religious tax for the support of teachers belonging to their denomination. As the years passed, Baptists and other dissenters increased their attacks on the establishment. Finally, in 1831, the state legislature approved a bill of disestablishment which was ratified in a constitutional amendment two years later. With that act, the last American establishment passed quietly into history.

On the national scene the Constitutional Convention, which met at Philadelphia in May 1787, gave little attention to the question of religion. Article VI contains the only direct reference to religion in the body of the Constitution. It provides that "no religious test shall ever be required as a qualification to any office of public trust under the United States." Many Baptists and Presbyterians favored the article but

---

[1] Quoted in A. P. Stokes, *Church and State in the United States*, Vol. I (New York: Harper & Brothers, c. 1950), p. 418.

felt that it should be made stronger through the addition of a Bill of Rights which would guarantee religious liberty and provide for disestablishment.

After ratification of the Constitution, support for additional guarantees of rights on a national level mounted steadily. The First Amendment to the Constitution in the Bill of Rights, adopted by Congress in 1789 and ratified two years later, was pertinent to religion. It provided that

> Congress shall make no law respecting an establishment of religion, or prohibiting the free exercise thereof; or abridging the freedom of speech, or of the press; or the right of the people peaceably to assemble and to petition the Government for a redress of grievances.

The purpose of the amendment was to discourage rivalry among the denominations for governmental favors and to prevent any national establishment, whether of a denominational or nondenominational character. It was designed not to protect Americans from religion but to insure the vitality and strengthening of religion; the experience of its framers was that state support tended to further complacency and thus render a denomination's efforts ineffectual.

## THE IMPACT OF RATIONAL RELIGION

The period immediately following the Revolution witnessed a progressive deterioration of spiritual zeal. The protracted conflict had been fought with cruelty and frequent disdain for even the rights of noncombatants. All the evils which ordinarily follow after war became manifest. Nor was the religious situation enhanced by liberal tendencies which had already crept into organized religion. Before Lexington and Concord, a strong reaction had asserted itself against the great revival. Tides of revolt from orthodoxy were rising and Deism was finding numerous advocates throughout the country.

Few colleges did not succumb to the new intellectual fever. Lyman Beecher, describing Yale College during the 1790's, wrote that "most of the classes before me were infidels, and called each other Voltaire, Rousseau, D'Alembert." The statement might have applied equally to classes from Dartmouth to the University of Georgia. Everywhere morals declined and discipline lagged. It was a period of transition, even upheaval, and if a devil-may-care attitude was common among the college generation, it was at least symbolic of the times.

To the orthodox ministry, persons of Deistic inclination were atheists, infidels, and agents of the prince of darkness. They stormed and raged against the "heretics" and charged them with committing every imaginable crime against society. Among conservative New Englanders, nothing too contemptuous could be said of Thomas Jefferson; he was the embodiment of all they held to be insidious both in politics and religion, a Francophile who could be expected to breed Jacobin radicalism. Other favorite whipping boys of the Protestant clergy were Ethan Allen and Thomas Paine, both of whom believed in God but rejected religious doctrines which were not grounded in reason.

The churches were not immune to the chilling effects of religious indifference. Attendance at services of worship declined noticeably, and many congregations averaged no more than four or five new members a year. In many parts of the South, Sunday became a day of "riot and drunkenness." The Presbyterian General Assembly of 1798 noted with apprehension "a general dereliction of religious principles and practices among our fellow citizens . . . and an abounding infidelity, which in many instances tends to atheism itself."

Conditions were no better on the frontier. The wild and reckless existence which faced the pioneer was a natural deterrent to inhibition, an invitation to moral laxity in the form of drunkenness and debauchery. Besides, the material concerns of the settler were necessarily so great that there seemed to be little time for cultivating the spiritual life. Nor did the inroads of Deism encourage churchmanship. According to the report of a pioneer in Kentucky around the turn of the century, half of the state's inhabitants subscribed to Deism. What was needed to stem the tide of spiritual diffidence was a revival of dynamic faith, a resurgence of religious vitality which could appeal to the heart as well as the mind. Such a revival would be forthcoming in the Second Awakening.

## CHURCH REORGANIZATION IN THE NATIONAL ERA

The changes which took place in the political order through the achievement of American independence gave rise to numerous challenges and opportunities for the forces of organized religion. Some denominations, having been bound tightly to ecclesiastical authorities in England, found that the severance of political ties necessitated a fresh appraisal of their positions. Religious bodies which had already attained full or partial autonomy discovered the wisdom of making certain structural changes by way of adjustment to a society in rapid transition. All saw the need to rethink their programs and to energize their institutions.

The Church of England in America faced the opening of the national period in a sorry and uncertain condition. In the states north of Maryland a large percentage of the clergy, being Loyalists, soon departed the country. In the South the loss of special privileges through disestablishment and the potent opposition of dissenters contributed to widespread defections to other denominations and the subsequent weakening of the church.

A principal and necessary concern among Episcopalians was the establishment of an American episcopate. In Connecticut, ten clergymen met in March 1783, and commissioned Samuel Seabury (1729-1796) to go to England for episcopal consecration. When the English bishops refused to proceed with his consecration unless he would take an oath of allegiance to the English crown, Seabury traveled northward to Scotland where he was greeted warmly by the non-juring bishops (successors of those bishops who in 1688 had refused to take the oath of allegiance to William and Mary). These bishops conferred episcopal consecration on him in November 1784.

Meanwhile state conventions of the clergy had chosen William White and Samuel Provoost to become bishops of Pennsylvania and New York, respectively; and plans had been made for the calling of a General Convention to meet in Philadelphia during September 1785. Sixteen clergymen and twenty-four laymen, representing seven states, were present at the opening of the Convention; the New England churches sent no delegates. The principal work of the Convention, over which William White presided, was to frame an Ecclesiastical Constitution and to direct an appeal to the English bishops that they confer episcopal orders upon the men chosen by the state conventions. As soon as Parliament had passed the necessary act of permission, White and Provoost sailed to England and were consecrated in Lambeth Chapel in February 1787. With three bishops now in America, the canonical number required for the consecration of other bishops, there could no longer be any question as to the ability of the American church to perpetuate itself.

When the General Convention met in July 1789, Seabury was present; two months later, at a second session, delegates from the New England states joined the assembly and signed a revised constitution which provided for a separate House of Bishops. The accomplishments of this Convention were little short of extraordinary. Not only did it achieve church unity, but it adopted a constitution and set of canons and authorized a revised Book of Common Prayer. It set the course which the church would follow for decades to come.

Until the close of the Revolution, the Methodist movement in America remained identified with the Anglican Church, being simply a part of the "Wesleyan Connection." Yet, as early as May 1779, a group of southern preachers met at Fluvanna, Virginia, and decided to establish a presbytery and ordain ministers so that the people might be provided with the sacraments. For a time it appeared that there might be a schism between them and the northern faction which remained loyal to Francis Asbury. Fortunately the two groups were able to reconcile their differences; the southern wing recognized Asbury as General Assistant and agreed to abstain from administering the sacraments.

After the restoration of peace, Wesley reestablished connections with his brethren in the United States, with a view of resuming full authority over them. Knowing their need of ministers, Wesley invited his friend, Dr. Thomas Coke, a presbyter in the Church of England, to receive ordination as a superintendent at his hands; he also arranged for the ordination of two other men as presbyters. The action was contrary to the canons of the Church of England, but Wesley justified it on the ground that in the ancient church of Alexandria presbyters had ordained bishops. In July 1784, he appointed Coke, Richard Whatcoat, and Thomas Vasey to service in America.

Upon his arrival in New York in November 1784, Coke met with Asbury; the result of this meeting was the calling of a ministerial conference at Baltimore on December 24, 1784. At the "Christmas Conference" the delegates resolved to organize as the Methodist Episcopal Church. Both Asbury and Coke were recognized as superintendents; but after 1785, Coke spent little time in the United States and Asbury assumed practical command, even to the extent of assigning to himself the title of bishop. Another contribution of the Conference was the adoption of a form of government and discipline. The organization was highly centralized, basic units being those of the circuit and the conference. In the matter of doctrine, the Conference approved twenty-four Articles of Religion, adapted from the thirty-nine of the Anglican Church, and added another article concerning the rulers of the United States.

Probably no religious body in America faced the national period with more privileges and more internal weaknesses than the Congregational. At the close of the Revolution it was the largest denomination in the country, with its strength centered in New England. Unfortunately, the blessings of temporal prosperity contributed to a spirit of phlegmatic complacency which unfitted the denomination to meet the challenges presented by a burgeoning society. Failing to develop a broad outlook upon the work at hand, the Congregationalists sentenced themselves to remain essentially a sectional body during the formative stage of the country's history and to play a relatively minor role in the building of the West.

Since the founding of their first presbytery in 1706, American Presbyterians had been independent of European judicatories. Nevertheless, the rapid strides made by the denomination, which was the second largest in America, called for some reorganization which would enable the church to function more efficiently. To continue governing the church as a whole through the overgrown undelegated Synod was clearly absurd if not impossible.

The year 1788 proved to be one of decisive action. At the meeting of Synod, a Form of Government and Book of Discipline were adopted as the Constitution of the Presbyterian Church in America, together with the Westminster Confession of Faith which had been amended to conform to the American principle of the separation of church and state. It also adopted the amended Larger Catechism, the Shorter Catechism, and the Westminster Directory for the Worship of God. The Synod then directed its own dissolution and the creation of four synods and sixteen presbyteries under the national governance of a General Assembly. On May 31, 1789, at the very time the first United States Congress under the Federal Constitution was meeting at New York, the General Assembly convened at Philadelphia. Quite appropriately, the Assembly appointed a committee to draft a suitable address to President George Washington, to which Washington graciously responded. These mutual felicitations symbolized the advent of a new era which Presbyterians knew they could face with self-confidence now that their reorganization was complete.

No religious body greeted the national period with more anticipation than the Baptists. With the removal of whatever stigmas had been attached to their communion, they made rapid gains from Maine to Georgia. In Virginia they led all other denominations in numerical strength; throughout the nation they stood in third place. While their polity did not seem to warrant a national organization, the spirit of the times led them to a greater appreciation of cooperation between churches. From 1751 to 1799, forty-nine voluntary associations came into existence. They had no more than advisory powers, but they made their influence felt and with most beneficial effects.

Through the work of Henry M. Muhlenberg the Lutheran Church in America had gradually acquired a semblance of organization. The first stage in the process was reached in 1761 when the Ministerium of Pennsylvania, an annual assembly of the clergy, was brought into being. Gradually a synodical constitution was formed; and in 1781, it was formally approved under the title "The Evangelical Lutheran Ministerium in North America." Additional synods were organized in New York in 1786, North Carolina in 1803, and Ohio in 1818. At the same time a national union movement was developing, the result being the organization of the General Synod in 1820, at Hagerstown, Maryland. This Synod was given large advisory powers and was authorized to plan missionary and educational programs on a national level. It would prove to be a highly effective force in welding the heterogeneous elements which made up American Lutheranism.

At the close of the Revolutionary era, Roman Catholicism in America found itself in a relatively strong position. Many Roman Catholics had done yeoman service in the struggle against England, and this had done much to elevate their general prestige. Nevertheless, devout churchmen could scarcely face the national era with giddy optimism. The church had serious problems, most of which were internal. There were less than thirty priests to minister to a Roman Catholic population of more than 24,000, centered largely in Maryland and Pennsylvania.

What was needed was a man of deep insight who would give leadership and direction to the church. That man was to be found in Father John Carroll (1735-1815), a Jesuit, who held the office of Prefect Apostolic from 1784 to 1789. Throughout this period he was troubled by problems of discipline of the clergy and the practice of lay trusteeship, in which lay members not only held title to church property but frequently tried to control the affairs of the parish.

It was obvious that episcopal powers were needed to avert schism in the church and this was recognized by Rome. The American priests were given the right to choose their own bishop and they elected John Carroll, who sailed for England and was consecrated Bishop of Baltimore by the Vicar-Apostolic of London on August 15, 1790. But the problem of lay trusteeship did not cease after Carroll's elevation to episcopal rank. Roman Catholic laymen had become so accustomed to the privilege of conducting their own parochial affairs that they were reluctant to relinquish it. The circumstances were such that Bishop Carroll could do little more than concede the right of trusteeship to the laity, at least for the time being. During the early nineteenth century, debate on this issue would rise to gigantic proportions.

Another serious problem which faced Carroll and his successors was that of staffing the parishes. After the Revolution, it was difficult to secure English priests for work in America. The great influx of priests was from France, where life had been difficult for the clergy in the secularized order which followed the French Revolution. Though their efforts were largely ineffective, due partially to opposition on the part of Irish congregations, some of them rose to high offices in the church. But this was merely a temporary arrangement. The real future lay with the Irish priests, scores of whom entered the United States in the early nineteenth century.

Steady gains by the church soon made it necessary to make changes in organization. In 1808, Pope Pius VII raised Baltimore to metropolitan status, with John Carroll as archbishop, and erected the four episcopal sees of Boston, New York, Philadelphia, and Bardstown, Kentucky. The church was at last becoming equipped to meet the challenge of an expanding America.

# CHAPTER SEVEN

# Church Expansion
# and the Second Awakening

It was Emerson who noted that "Europe extends to the Alleghenies, while America lies beyond." In the Middle West, a new pattern developed almost independently of the eastern models which looked to Europe for their inspiration. Though Spanish and French adventurers had sailed up its arbor-framed rivers and traversed its rolling or flat terrain, the stamp of Old World culture left but a faint impression upon the land, and this was obliterated by the ponderous tread of the American frontiersman. On the frontier this scion of individualism and progress carved out a new civilization, wild and crude according to urban standards, yet founded upon the dignity of man and his infinite perfectibility.

As time passed, the congested cities of the East looked increasingly toward the West. The very destiny of the nation seemed to depend on the events which transpired on the burgeoning frontier. It was through western expansion that the mighty nation, the affluent society, the Kingdom of God in America was to be achieved.

According to the terms of the Treaty of Peace with Great Britain in 1783, the territorial holdings of the United States were extended to the Mississippi. Persons of conservative inclination doubted whether the land would ever be fully settled; even the eastern seaboard had not fully succumbed to the onward press of civilization. Nevertheless, the rapid increase of population in a society plagued by economic depression dictated the establishment of new communities and the steady thrust of the frontier westward.

When the Revolution ended, the only settlements in the Ohio Valley were in western Pennsylvania, Kentucky, and Tennessee. North of the Ohio River the Indians were in almost complete possession. In

61

the region south of the Ohio, a steady wave of settlers poured into the wilderness. By 1829, nine of the eleven new states admitted to the Union were situated west of the Alleghenies and contained more than a third of the nation's population.

Diplomatic considerations played a significant role in the settlement of the West. The presence of the Spanish and later the French in the Mississippi Valley was regarded by the national government and settlers on the frontier as a threat to American expansion. Thus the French proposal in 1803 to sell the whole of Louisiana was accepted with dispatch by American diplomats. By this action the area of the United States was more than doubled, a political menace was removed, and the way was opened for unlimited colonization in the West.

## CHURCH EXTENSION IN THE WEST

Colonization of the West created special problems for organized religion. If the future of the nation depended upon what took place beyond the Appalachians, then the building of the Kingdom of God in America rested upon the ability of the churches to make an impact on frontier society. It was not simply a matter of sending ministers to care for relocated communicants; primarily it involved the conversion of countless persons who were unchurched.

From the standpoint of numbers, leadership, and prestige, the Congregationalists were the most important denomination in the country at the dawn of the national era. But no communion was less prepared to face the problems of the frontier. The preservation of the establishment in New England served to infect Congregationalists of that area with an attitude of self-centered complacency. More serious was the parochial viewpoint of their leaders who were so engrossed in the glories of New England that in their myopia they failed to envision a great nation extending to the Pacific. If the denomination had been able to render an adequate ministry to the 800,000 persons who, between 1790 and 1830, migrated from New England to frontier territory, it would undoubtedly have continued as one of the largest in the country. Failing in this, the Congregational Church was consigned to a minor role on the frontier.

Meanwhile, Presbyterians were active in the West; by the close of the Revolution they had planted churches in western Pennsylvania, Kentucky, and Tennessee. A boon to development in the West was their Plan of Union with the Congregationalists in 1801. For some decades the two denominations had gradually been drawing together; in 1791, the General Association of Connecticut and the Presbyterian General

Assembly agreed to send delegates to the meetings of the other. The General Associations of Vermont, New Hampshire, and Massachusetts later entered into a similar relationship with the Presbyterian Assembly.

During the great revival of 1798-1801, the Presbyterians sent missionaries into the frontier regions of New York, where they encountered Congregational ministers who had recently arrived from New England. Sensing the futility of competition, Jonathan Edwards the Younger, president of Union College, proposed the Plan of Union which was adopted in 1801. According to its terms, it was possible for Congregationalists and Presbyterians to form one congregation which might be connected with both denominations yet could conduct its local government as its members preferred. The church might call as its pastor a minister of either denomination. The practical effect of the alliance was the absorption of Congregational churches into Presbyterianism; this contributed to a growing estrangement between the two bodies. The so-called "Presbygational" system was impractical inasmuch as it brought together two autonomous denominations with distinct and often dissimilar doctrines and practices and subjected them to the impossible maintenance of a two-sided structure. That both sides abrogated the Plan of Union prior to the outbreak of the Civil War was hardly surprising.

By 1850, the Congregationalists, who at the close of the Revolution had ranked first among the American churches, had fallen to fourth place among Protestants with 197,000 members. The Presbyterians, with a membership of 487,000, had dropped from second to third place. For the Congregationalists, lack of a national view and policy was a contributing factor. For the Presbyterians, a major consideration was the failure to adapt their polity and practices to the needs of the frontier. Repudiation of emotional excesses in revivalism weakened their effectiveness among backwoodsmen. Their insistence upon an educated ministry meant that fewer men could qualify for missionary labors; and even though they used a circuit system, they still could not supply enough ministers to meet the demand.

Until the close of the War of 1812, the Protestant Episcopal Church was engaged principally in efforts to overcome the shock sustained by its losses in the Revolution. The church underwent a complete reorganization, but it was difficult to convince Americans that it was anything other than an English institution. With the withdrawal of the Methodists, the church was left with virtually no activities on the frontier.

During the early nineteenth century the Episcopal Church made significant progress in the frontier region of New York; elsewhere the gains were negligible. Nor was the situation greatly improved with the consecration, in 1835, of a missionary bishop for the West. The religious pattern for that area had already been established. By 1850, the Episcopal Church, with 90,000 communicants, had fallen from fourth to seventh place among Protestants. The factors which hindered the growth of Congregationalism and Presbyterianism were also operative in the Episcopal Church. The relative impotence of the church in ministering to the religious needs of frontier society can be attributed to the fact that the clergy were attached completely to their parishes, thus ruling out any wide practice of itinerancy.

Among the new stream of immigrants that flooded Kentucky and Tennessee were large numbers of Baptists who had been forced by economic depression to leave homes in the East. The greater majority originated in Virginia or North Carolina and belonged to the lower middle class. There was an aura of democracy about them which was diffused osmotically in the social and political mores and in the practice of religion. Their ministers were for the most part theologically untrained farmers who had felt a call to preach. And sermons were of the people and for the people, speaking to the condition of the frontiersman in a way which could never be matched by the cultivated clergyman from the East.

Baptist successes on the frontier may be attributed to the simple but efficient manner of their leaders. Unimpeded by ecclesiastical machinery, they could gather congregations and found churches wherever it seemed practical. To be sure there was organization. Most of the churches held monthly business meetings; all provided rules for administration and discipline. Strictness of discipline, however, seems not to have lessened their popularity. Indeed, Baptists were successful not only in holding their own members but in winning unchurched pioneers. By 1885, they stood second among Protestants in numerical strength throughout the nation with a total membership of 1,105,546.

At first sight, it might appear that the highly centralized and regulated Methodist system would have little appeal to democratically inclined frontiersmen. This liability was overcome by the effectiveness of the circuit system, a method introduced by Wesley to meet the religious needs of a shifting English population. Circuits established in newly settled areas always covered a wide territory, sometimes requiring six weeks to make the rounds. When a circuit rider came to a settlement which he deemed ripe for conversion, he preached to the people in any available place; if possible, he organized a class of a few believers and appointed a class leader to guide their spiritual progress during his absence. Members who felt a call to preach and demonstrated some ability in public speaking were encouraged to apply for a local preacher's license which entitled them to deliver sermons and organize classes. Thus the means was provided for a vital ministry to the unchurched as well as to professing Methodists.

In 1792, the position of presiding elder was created for overseeing the circuits and circuit riders in a given district. By 1796, the denomination had grown to such an extent that it was necessary to divide the country into six annual conferences, one of which served the territory west of the mountains. During the next half century, it became increasingly apparent that Methodist circuit riders were performing an efficacious work. By 1855, the national membership of Methodism was 1,577,014, making Methodists the largest Protestant body in the United States.

After 1787, large numbers of Friends moved into the Northwest Territory from Pennsylvania, Maryland, Virginia, the Carolinas, and Georgia. One principal motivating factor behind the Quaker migration was the desire to dwell in a territory where slavery was forbidden. By 1845, there were 18,000 Friends in Ohio and 30,000 in Indiana. Nevertheless, the Friends failed to make significant gains on the frontier essentially because they remained a static and exclusive body and thus made little impact on the outside world.

Before the end of the eighteenth century, certain Roman Catholic refugee priests were being sent across the Alleghenies to serve the long-overlooked French settlements at Vincennes and Kaskaskia. Others were being sent to minister to newly formed communities in Kentucky. An appointment in the West was regarded at once as a challenge and a remarkable opportunity by many of the French priests who had encountered indifference or opposition on the Atlantic Coast. By 1808, the number of the church's adherents living west of the Alleghenies had increased to such an extent that a new diocese was erected at Bardstown, Kentucky. Father Benedict Flaget became its first bishop.

With the purchase of Louisiana in 1803, 15,000 Roman Catholics of French and Spanish descent came under the government of the United States. For the time being the Holy See placed them under the care of Bishop Carroll, an impossible task considering his already burdensome duties. In 1812, William du Bourg was appointed as Administrator Apostolic of Louisiana and the Floridas; three years later he became bishop of the Diocese of New Orleans. In 1827, the northern part of this diocese was separated from New Orleans and formed into the Diocese of St. Louis.

## THE RESURGENCE OF REVIVALISM

Just before the close of the eighteenth century the conditions which had brought religious life in the new nation to a low ebb were gradually replaced by forces which promoted a revival of faith. French rationalism had suffered a crippling defeat through American indignation over the Reign of Terror. With its passing there was ushered in a new age of romantic idealism, an age of the common man, of popular democracy and crusading evangelism. America's spiritual recovery began with the Second Awakening.

As early as 1786, signs of a forthcoming revival were abroad in the South. At Hampden-Sidney College and Washington College, in Virginia, there was an awakening among the student body and a number of decisions to enter the ministry. In New England the way was prepared chiefly by the doctrine and preaching of evangelical Congregationalists in the Edwardean tradition. In 1791, there was an awakening at North Yarmouth, Maine; the next year it was extended to towns in Massachusetts and Connecticut. Year by year the revival increased in strength until reaching its full flowering in 1799.

The theology of the revival reflected the new spirit of democracy. It stood for the sovereignty of God, but departed from Calvinism in its emphasis upon the work of man. The Arminian tendencies of Unitarianism and Methodism undoubtedly influenced the change which was demanded by the spirit of the times. In any case, the classic doctrine of divine election was relegated to the background and men were assured that all who sought salvation might find it through a vital faith and works of righteousness.

The frontier phase of the Second Awakening was characterized by frenzied excitement and emotional outbursts, even physical aberrations. Yet there were times when it exhibited dignity and order, especially in the older and more settled communities. As conducted by Presbyterians and Congregationalists, it offered salvation to the elect alone; thus its range of influence was limited. As conducted by Methodists and Baptists, it offered salvation, mainly on an emotional basis, to all who would accept Christ in faith. It attracted so many people that it was frequently necessary to hold the great revival meetings out of doors in order to accommodate the surging throngs.

The Cane Ridge camp meeting of August 1801, proved to be the colossus of revival meetings in Kentucky. People flocked from all parts of the surrounding country to attend what promised to be a truly remarkable occasion. The meeting, which had been set up under Presbyterian auspices, turned out to be an interdenominational enterprise with Baptist and Methodist preachers joining enthusiastically in the proceedings. As fiery-tongued evangelists poured out impassioned appeals for hardened sinners to become "washed in the blood of the Lamb," scores fell prostrate before them, writhing in agony. Others would occasionally rush to their feet and proclaim the wonders of redemption in stentorian tones that would cause the most fearless frontiersman to tremble. Between the years 1800 and 1804, the revival spread like wildfire through Kentucky, Tennessee, Ohio, western New York and Pennsylvania, the old South, and western New England.

The revival blew hot and cold. In the Presbyterian camp it was greeted with mingled feelings of approbation and contempt. Baptists and Methodists had no reservations. To such leaders as Bishop Asbury the camp meeting became Methodism's harvest time. As the years passed there was less cooperation with Presbyterians until the revivals came to be characterized by denominational exclusiveness. Even the hymns revealed a growing spirit of sectarianism, as in this favorite of Methodist evangelists:

> The *world,* the *Devil* and *Tom Paine*
> Have try'd their force, but all in vain,
> They can't prevail, the reason is,
> The Lord Defends the Methodist.

By the 1840's, revivalism had passed its peak of popularity in the trans-Allegheny West and was entering a period of decline.

To understand the effect of the revival one must bear in mind the prevailing social conditions. Here was a population transplanted into a wild region where there were few social restrictions due to convention or civil law. Suddenly they were convicted with a sense of their culpability before God. This was accomplished not by a gradual educational process but through an intensive revival campaign which lasted for days. As multitudes of people were pressed together, engaged in the task of contemplating momentous truths which were being communicated through impassioned repetition, there was bound to be a buildup of tension which would have to be released. This explains the sudden outcries, hysterical weeping, faintings, and trances.

That transformation of character was short-lived among some persons converted at the revivals must be freely conceded; on the other hand, others demonstrated lasting moral improvement as a result of their experience. With all its excesses, the revival was religiously constructive, leaving a positive influence which would not be effaced from American society for years to come.

## The Great Missionary Enterprise

The Peace of Ghent, which rang down the curtain on the most doubtful military victory in American history, demonstrated that the future of the United States as an independent nation was assured. It also presaged the rise of a powerful nationalistic spirit. As Americans looked toward the frontier, the breeding ground of nationalism, they dreamed that their "manifest destiny" was the conquest of that gigantic sweep of territory which plunged westward to greet the ocean. The accession of Florida, Texas, Oregon, and California was the dream translated into reality.

The new spirit of nationalism also had an impact upon organized religion. Many clergymen of insight saw that in time the strength of the country would lie west of the Allegheny Mountains. They became convinced that the churches would have to develop strong missionary programs if frontier society was to be won to Christian ideals and practices. Through missions the West, the nation, and ultimately the world might be redeemed from the disastrous effects of immorality, skepticism, and materialism.

Various theological and philosophical forces helped to prepare the way for the great missionary enterprise. One of the more important was renewed emphasis upon the dignity and worth of man. Coupled with the natural rights philosophy and Jeffersonian individualism, the concept of the worth of man tended to awaken more interest in human advancement and thus indirectly aided the cause of missions. More direct support came from the Arminian doctrine of God's infinite love and mercy for all men, which could become universally known only through the extension of missions. Equally influential was the disinterested benevolence theory of New England Congregationalist Samuel Hopkins. He believed that since God wills the greatest good for the greatest number, the true Christian will sacrifice his personal interests for the greater good of the whole. To many persons this constituted a call to dedicate their lives to mission work among the "heathen." When these ideas were charged with the electric excitement of the Second Awakening, the American missionary movement sprang to life.

At the close of the War of 1812, the new nationalistic spirit seemed to call for a program of home missions on a national level. The most important of these new national agencies was the American Home Missionary Society, founded in 1826 by delegates from the Presbyterian, Congregational, Dutch Reformed, and Associate Reformed denominations. Its work was centered largely in the areas north of Virginia, Kentucky, and Tennessee; this can be explained partially by the fact that most of its missionaries came from states north of Maryland and preferred to work among people of similar background. Many of them had a natural bias against functioning in regions where slavery was practiced.

On the whole, missionaries of the society had little respect for their Baptist and Methodist competitors, regarding them as untutored and incompetent. Flavel Bascom, who came to Illinois in 1833, mentions the preaching of a rustic evangelist who "went bellowing and blowing through the Bible shedding no more light upon the passages quoted, than the roar of artillery does upon our declaration of independence." Conversely, the Methodist circuit rider, Peter Cartwright, had harsh words for young missionaries sent out "to civilize and Christianize the poor heathen of the West." Yet in spite of rivalries and clashes, frontier religion manifested a certain unity and unusual tolerance. An attitude of forbearance and cooperation was made mandatory by the very want of resources which plagued frontier society.

While the Presbyterians were officially connected with the American Home Missionary Society, after 1816 they also worked through their own Board of Missions. By 1828, they had become established in most states east of the Mississippi and in Missouri, Oklahoma, Arkansas, and Louisiana. In 1817, the General Missionary (Triennial) Convention of the Baptist Denomination in the United States, organized in 1814, began to send missionaries to preach in the new western settlements. The Methodists founded a national missionary society in 1819, the Episcopalians in 1821.

The painful experiences of Indian wars on the frontier combined with the revival of missionary interest in the national era persuaded many Christian leaders of the necessity of Indian missions. By 1823, the Methodists had a mission among the Potawatomies in northern Illinois; in little more than a decade the work had been extended to include the Winnebagos and Western Chippewas in Wisconsin. In the South several denominations were engaged, by 1830, in conducting missions among the Cherokees in Tennessee and Arkansas, the Choctaws and Chickasaws in Georgia and Mississippi, and the Creeks and Osages in Arkansas and Missouri. During the 1830's and 1840's, mission work was inaugurated in the Pacific Northwest by Presbyterians Marcus Whitman and Henry Spalding and by the Jesuit father Pierre-Jean De Smet.

In the national era Christian missions to the Negro were greatly augmented. The great majority of Christianized Negroes affiliated with the Baptist and Methodist churches, largely because they held the greatest emotional appeal. It has been estimated that of the 468,000 Negroes in the South who were church members in 1859, 215,000 were Methodists and 175,000 were Baptists. While thousands of Negroes belonged to white congregations, there was a growing demand during the early nineteenth century for churches of their own. The Negro church performed a social function of which a mixed or white congregation would have been incapable. It presented a gospel of hope focused upon a more glorious life beyond the grave and thus provided a measure of security for a people continually beset with frustration and despair.

A growing racial consciousness among Negroes led to a demand for independent denominations. It was based on social and anthropological considerations rather than theological differences. In 1816, delegates from several Negro congregations met in Philadelphia and organized what became the African Methodist Episcopal Church. This body adopted substantially the discipline of the Methodist Episcopal Church. Another Negro denomination, the African Methodist Episcopal Church Zion, was founded in 1821.

The same forces which prompted the rise of home missionary interest, when combined with certain other distinctive forces, gave powerful impetus to the development of foreign missions. Toward the end of the eighteenth century stirring reports of the missionary accomplishments of the English Baptist cobbler, William Carey, in India, were brought to America. The news was greeted with a sense of admiration but more profoundly by the realization that the United States would have to act quickly if the world was to be won to Christ through its example and preaching.

To American Protestants it seemed quite clear that God had chosen them to be the political and religious teachers of the human race. The fact that every day more and more Europeans were arriving in America, the land of opportunity, bore testimony to their recognition that in the United States lay the hope of the world. The keynote of American history was progress—the upward climb to a higher order of civilization which might in turn be shared with the less fortunate nations.

New England seamen who had participated in the increasing American trade with the Orient, together with tourists who had visited the Far East, helped to spark the foreign missions movement by their exotic tales of life on that distant continent. In 1806, Samuel J. Mills (1783-1818), a young Congregationalist who felt called to become a foreign missionary, matriculated at Williams College. He and several other students formed a band pledged to the work of missions. In 1810, some of this group, now enrolled in Andover Seminary, requested the Congregational General Association of Massachusetts to sponsor them as missionaries. The result was the formation in that year of the American Board of Commissioners for Foreign Missions. Two years later Adoniram Judson, Luther Rice, and three other men set sail for India as agents of the Board. En route to the Orient, Judson and Rice were converted to Baptist principles and, upon their arrival in Calcutta, were immersed. In order that he and Judson might receive adequate support, Rice returned to America and toured the country organizing local missionary societies. Then in May 1814, the General Missionary Convention of the Baptist Denomination in the United States of America for Foreign Missions was founded in Philadelphia.

Meanwhile, the American Board had been establishing missions in Ceylon and the Hawaiian Islands; before 1860, its missionary program was extended to include stations in China, Greece, Syria, and South Africa. In 1837, the Old School Presbyterian Church organized a Board of Foreign Missions which carried on missionary programs in Africa, India, Siam, China, and South America. The Missionary and Bible Society of the Methodist Episcopal Church was founded in 1819; by the 1830's, it was sending missionaries to Liberia and South America. In 1821, the Protestant Episcopal Church organized its Domestic and Foreign Missionary Society and initiated programs in West Africa, China, and Greece. The Foreign Missionary Society of the Evangelical Lutheran Church in the United States was founded in 1837.

While the earliest missionaries seem to have entered upon their foreign assignments with no thought of accomplishing more than the conversion of the "heathen," as the nineteenth century progressed, more attention was given to missions as a means of imparting the American way of life. In Hawaii, for example, the program of missions was a door which opened the way to commerce and finally to political control by the United States. Before the nineteenth century ended, the foreign missions enterprise would have proved itself an unusually important, if sometimes unconscious, ally of American imperialism.

## DEVELOPMENTS IN CHRISTIAN EDUCATION

One of the important by-products of the Age of Disinterested Benevolence was a passion for learning. Up and down the country, church leaders, especially those of the Congregationalist, Presbyterian, or Episcopal persuasions, were recognizing that sound education was one of the prerequisites to a Christian America, that only through training could the citizenry adequately prepare for their divine mission to the world. The dearth of educated ministers alone dictated the immediate necessity of acquiring additional institutions for their preparation.

The first permanently located theological institution founded on a complete plan was established by orthodox Congregationalists at Andover, Massachusetts, in 1807. It came about as the result of Harvard College's steady drift toward Unitarianism. The motivation for seminary founding, therefore, was based not only on the need for ministers but on the demand that their training be in harmony with the views of their denomination. The Presbyterians opened their first seminary at Princeton in 1812; the Lutherans established Hartwick Seminary at Otsego, New York, in 1816; the Episcopalians founded General Theological Seminary in New York in 1817. Divinity schools in connection with Harvard and Yale universities were established in 1816 and 1822 respectively.

Despite the suspicion of an educated ministry exhibited by Methodists and Baptists, both denominations established seminaries prior to 1840. The reason lay not only in increased demand by the laity for a clergy that could command their respect but also in the competition presented by Congregationalists and Presbyterians. The establishment of Newton Theological Seminary in Massachusetts by the Baptists in 1825, and a seminary by the Methodists in Newbury, Vermont, in 1839, represents the first efforts of these denominations to alleviate their educational deficiency.

The first true Presbyterian seminary in the West was Western, established at Pittsburgh in 1827. Lane Theological Seminary, founded at Cincinnati in 1832, was operated under the Presbyterian-Congregationalist Plan of Union. In 1824, the Episcopalians established Bexley Hall in Ohio as their first theological school in the West.

Early in the national period a number of forces combined to influence an unprecedented wave of college building under the auspices of American churches. The immediate causes were the desire to train candidates for the ministry, the competition between denominations, and the fear of ascending Roman Catholic power. The first factor was operative primarily among Presbyterians, Congregationalists, and Episcopalians, who concerned themselves with an educated clergy. Neither Baptists nor Methodists regarded their earliest colleges first and foremost as schools for ministerial training. That they organized colleges at all was due partially to their resentment over Congregational and Presbyterian competition on the frontier. Concern over the phenomenal increase in Roman Catholic population through immigration during the 1830's and 1840's led to a further demand for church colleges.

The achievements of the churches in the area of college building prior to the Civil War were no less than astounding. Between 1780 and 1860, the number of colleges in the United States increased from 9 to 173 which survived and perhaps four times that number which became defunct. Most of these were operated by the several denominations. The Presbyterians controlled 49 colleges, the Congregationalists 21. The Roman Catholics founded 14 institutions, the Episcopalians 11, the Lutherans 6, the Disciples of Christ 5, the German Reformed and Universalists 4 each, the Friends and Unitarians 2 each, and the Dutch Reformed and United Brethren 1 each. The Baptists, who had only 4 colleges in 1830, increased that number to 25 by 1860; in the same period, the Methodists founded their first 34 institutions of higher learning. These colleges were administered and staffed mainly by ministers.

In 1780, Robert Raikes, a philanthropist who lived in Gloucester, England, initiated an interesting educational experiment. On Sundays, he gathered a number of indigent children and gave them elementary education as well as specifically religious instruction. The Sunday School movement soon spread to America. In most cases the schools, while promoted by Christians, were administered independently of the church organization by societies and unions. The first organization of this kind originated in Philadelphia in 1790 and was known as the First Day or Sabbath School Society. Other large cities such as Pittsburgh, Boston, New York, Baltimore, and Charleston followed suit.

The spirit of nationalism contributed to a growing demand for a Sunday School movement on a national level. The result was the organization of the American Sunday School Union in May 1824. The Union, which was strictly an enterprise for laymen, was supported by all of the major denominations. Its principal function at first was to publish lesson materials which contained nothing offensive to any of the evangelical churches. This made it possible to set up schools in communities where no single denomination was strong enough to maintain a school of its own.

The early schools had four grades: infant, in which the alphabet and words of one syllable were mastered; elementary, in which words of two and three syllables were spelled; Scripture, in which portions of the Bible were read; and senior, in which there were readings from both testaments. At first the schools offered a combination of secular and religious instruction. However, as public schools improved, the Sunday School was gradually taken over by the church and the instruction made distinctively religious. Eventually the majority of Protestant denominations made the promotion and care of Sunday Schools part of their church activities.

The circulation of the Bible, particularly in the West, was also a concern of the churches. This work was conducted at first by state Bible societies; after 1816, the principal work was performed by the American Bible Society. The purpose of the society was to circulate Bibles "without note or comment" in all the nations of the earth. A kindred organization was the American Tract Society, founded in 1825. Its purpose was to spread the basic doctrines of evangelical Protestantism. Among the society's publications were devotional works, biographies, and classics. Tracts offered such inviting topics as "The Evils of Excessive Drinking" and "The Ruinous Consequences of Gambling."

Religious journals of a general nature also flooded the market. By 1840, the number of religious publications stood at 850; about half of these were denominational in character. While Presbyterians and Universalists led the field in publication, the Methodists were the first to issue an official publication, the *Methodist Magazine* (1818).

It would be difficult to overemphasize the contribution made by such publications in the molding of American thought. They represented one of the primary means of bringing Christian education into the home and influencing the lives of thousands in a positive way.

# CHAPTER EIGHT

# Patterns of Religious Diversification

While Americans cooperated in a score of spiritual enterprises at the opening of the nineteenth century, the heterogeneity of their religious institutions and life became more apparent as the century progressed. One force which promoted this trend was the individualistic character of the age, which nurtured an attitude of nonconformity and self-reliance and often manifested itself in liberal theologies which stood adamantly against churchly or Biblical authoritarianism; another was a strong sectarian spirit, encouraged by diverse interpretations of the Bible.

## Liberal Trends in New England

From the middle of the eighteenth century an increasing array of liberal ideas made an appearance in New England Congregationalism. Many ministers in eastern Massachusetts, particularly those who had opposed the revival, began to espouse a rational religion devoid of Trinitarian concepts. The estrangement between them and their orthodox colleagues became steadily more pronounced after the election of a liberal candidate, Henry Ware, to the divinity professorship at Harvard in 1805. According to conservatives, the liberals held to the mere humanity of Christ. In reality they held to an Arian or supernatural position, while rejecting the doctrine of the Trinity.

In 1819, William Ellery Channing (1780-1842), a Boston minister, preached an ordination sermon before a Unitarian society in Baltimore; his subject was "Unitarian Christianity." In it he exalted the role of reason in perceiving revelation and interpreting the Bible. He rejected Trinitarianism and the orthodox concept of the atonement. Man might win salvation through the exercise of his moral faculties. The sermon, which was given national publicity, came to be regarded as the platform of the movement. The revolt fanned into full flame, and by 1825, 125 churches had formed the American Unitarian Association.

By the 1830's, a left-wing movement was developing within Unitarianism. It was intimately associated with a group of New England savants who founded the Transcendental Club. Among these literati, the shining star was Ralph Waldo Emerson (1803-1882). He believed that God incarnates Himself in every man just as He did in Jesus, and reveals Himself progressively from within. Each person must develop his own religion. Such Transcendentalism was antagonistic both to Congregationalism and the Channing type of Unitarianism.

For Theodore Parker (1810-1860), Boston pastor, religion was nothing more than morality, the love of man responding to the love of God. Such teaching evoked a storm of protest from more conservative Unitarians, and Parker soon found that many pulpits were closed to him. For half a century Unitarianism was torn by controversy over these conflicting theologies.

An emerging denomination often associated with Unitarianism was Universalism. Organized as a denomination in 1785, it emphasized the universal salvation of men but stood in basic theological agreement with Unitarianism.

The liberal forces which aided Unitarianism also exercised an influence on those who remained within the Congregational fold. They fostered a more optimistic view of man and his possibilities. As Nathaniel W. Taylor (1786-1858), first professor of Didactic Theology in Yale Divinity School, interpreted Calvinism, man's moral depravity is his own act. It is man's nature to do so. Men will persist in sinning until they are converted through the power of divine grace. But no irresistible force will bring them into a state of salvation against their wills. This teaching incurred the displeasure of both orthodox Congregationalists and Unitarians.

A prime exponent of the later New Haven Theology was Taylor's student, Horace Bushnell (1802-1876). In the book, *Christian Nurture* (1847), he rejected the idea of total depravity and insisted that a child is susceptible to good even though he is plagued by sinful tendencies from his birth. Christians should refrain from emphasizing the datable conversion experience and raise their children as part of the household of faith so that there should never be a time in their lives when they thought they were anything but Christians. Bushnell was accused of reducing Christianity to a form of religious naturalism. But the idea could not be effaced; rather, it became instrumental in inaugurating a new philosophy of religious education.

Of like importance to theology was Bushnell's representation of Christ as the expression of God in finite form, the revealer of the divine nature. He held that Christ came into the world to manifest the mercy and compassionate love of God. Men are saved not by the sacrifice of Christ as an act of propitiation to God but by a living spiritual union with their Lord, through whose suffering they come to know and respond to God's redemptive love. By 1900, this idea would have permeated liberal Protestant thought.

## THEOLOGICAL CONFLICTS ON THE FRONTIER

During the opening decades of the nineteenth century, religion on the frontier manifested a decidedly anti-Calvinist bias. Concepts of an aristocratic God who determines all things were not in keeping with the democratic and optimistic ideas of the frontier mind. But this was a period of individualism also, and no single expression of religion could meet the varied needs and interests of backwoodsmen. The result was that the older denominations had to face the competitive force of Presbyterian schismatic bodies which withdrew to form new ecclesiastical groupings.

The younger, more democratically inclined elements among the Presbyterian clergy in Kentucky and Tennessee had used revivalistic techniques and preached modified Calvinistic doctrines with some effectiveness. Unhappily, their apparent success had only served to widen the gap between the revivalistic and anti-revivalistic factions. The revival party saw that strict adherence to Presbyterian doctrine and practice would lead to permanent losses. Equally disturbing was the high educational standard for ordination, which caused the ministerial supply to be sharply curtailed. In 1802, the Cumberland Presbytery, in order to find at least a partial solution to these problems, licensed several persons without college training to preach. The Synod of Kentucky appointed a committee to examine the proceedings of Cumberland Presbytery; as a result of its findings, the presbytery was dissolved. Some of its ministers later organized an independent Cumberland Presbytery, in 1810, which became the nucleus of the Cumberland Presbyterian Church.

Another significant movement emerged under the leadership of Barton Warren Stone (1772-1844), a young revivalist preacher who had been ordained to the Presbyterian ministry, despite the fact that he could not affirm the doctrine of the Trinity. During the Second Awakening, he and several other ministers who were active in the Kentucky revivals came to doubt the doctrines of election and limited atonement. When the Synod of Kentucky, in 1803, brought two of them to trial for teaching Arminian doctrines, Stone and four other ministers seceded from the Synod and organized the independent Springfield Presbytery. The following year they published a pamphlet in which they argued for the Bible as the sole basis of doctrine. A few months later they reached the conclusion that the Presbyterian system was inadequate to bring about the desired unity of Christians. They therefore disbanded the presbytery and adopted the name "Christian" as an expression of their anti-sectarian convictions. By 1827, this new Christian Church, which stood for the independence of each local congregation, numbered nearly 13,000 communicants; a majority resided in Ohio, Kentucky, Tennessee, and Indiana.

At the same time the followers of Stone were promoting their cause, to the East was evolving a similar movement with which they would eventually merge. Its founder was Thomas Campbell (1763-1854), a Scotch-Irish Seceder Presbyterian minister. Upon his arrival in America in 1807, he affiliated with the Associate (Seceder) Synod of North America and was assigned to a circuit in southwestern Pennsylvania. When he invited all Christians to participate in the communion, regardless of denominational connection, he found himself in difficulty with his presbytery and finally withdrew to become a free-lance minister. In 1809, he and his followers organized the Christian Association of Washington; its motto was "Where the Scriptures speak, we speak; where the Scriptures are silent, we are silent."

Campbell's son, Alexander (1788-1866), arrived from Scotland in 1809; he took up the study of the Scriptures in the original languages and preached frequently in private houses. In 1811, when the association organized the Brush Run Church, Thomas Campbell was chosen elder and Alexander was ordained to the ministry. The church observed the Lord's Supper weekly and practiced immersion as the mode of baptism. In this way the church came into closer relations with the Baptists. By 1813, it had been received into the Redstone Baptist Association, a connection which it maintained until 1830.

To Alexander Campbell fell the task of building a definitive theology for the Disciples. Its cardinal feature was that with the coming of Christ the entire law had been abrogated; the principles of morality contained in the law were still in force, but only because they were necessary to any covenant beyond God and man. Christ introduced a completely new covenant, with its own institutions and ordinances.

In 1824, Campbell and Barton Stone met for the first time and immediately recognized that their programs had much in common. The intervening years brought a deepening sense of unity; and in 1832, leaders of the two groups made the decision to unite. Due to the nature of their church polity, merger could be accomplished merely by vote of the individual congregations. This was done with amazing alacrity, thanks to the effective and persuasive work of the leaders. Nevertheless, a number of Christian churches in the West and a majority of those in the East refused to enter the union.

## DENOMINATIONAL TENSIONS

As the spirit of sectionalism became increasingly characteristic of American life in the restless, tempestuous era which followed 1830, so a growing sectarianism typified the decline of the sense of community between and within the denominations. New sects arose amid the welter of confusion and emotionalism, while older communions bled from the wounds inflicted by bitter schisms. The Presbyterians were first to succumb to the forces of estrangement.

Almost from the outset, the Plan of Union had evoked dissension among Presbyterians with varying theological emphases. The strong winds of New England Congregational theology which surged through the Plan of Union churches seemed to orthodox or Old School Presbyterians of the Scotch-Irish tradition like the hot breath of Satan. In 1830, Albert Barnes, New School minister, became pastor of the First Presbyterian Church, Philadelphia. Since he held that a sinner is not "personally answerable for the transgressions of Adam," which was the same as denying the federal doctrine of imputed guilt, he was brought to trial for heresy but was finally acquitted by the General Assembly. Equally troublesome was the case of Lyman Beecher, president of Lane Seminary, who was charged before the Presbytery of Cincinnati, in 1834, with heresy in regard to the doctrines of original sin, human ability, and the regenerative activity of the Holy Spirit. His trial also ended in acquittal.

Orthodox Presbyterians were further discontent with the Plan of Union inasmuch as the churches organized under it could not be adequately controlled by Presbyterian courts. As for interdenominational agencies such as the American Home Missionary Society, the orthodox concluded that it would be best for Presbyterians to withdraw support from such agencies and found their own denominational boards under the authority of the General Assembly. A minor cause of tension was the slavery issue, as New School ministers were more aggressively opposed to slavery than those of the Old School.

At the General Assembly of 1837, the orthodox held a majority and were armed with a strategy to rid themselves of opponents. The result was that the Plan of Union was abrogated by the Assembly; and the four synods of Western Reserve, Utica, Geneva, and Genesee, which had been organized under the Plan of Union, were read out of the church.

The Assembly then voted to terminate cooperative activities with various interdenominational societies and create a Board of Foreign Missions. In 1838, the commissioners from the exscinded synods formed a General Assembly. The schism was complete; four-ninths of the original denomination constituted the New School Presbyterian Church.

As the years passed, the Old School Presbyterian Church progressively became less rigid in its doctrinal requirements. Its chief theologian was the Princeton scholar, Charles Hodge (1797-1878). He gave the federal theology a central place in his system and held to the verbal inspiration of the Bible. At the same time he revealed a slightly more liberal train of thought in allowing for some error in the ideas of the Biblical writers and insisting upon the salvation of all who die in infancy. His work paved the way for a less polemical spirit in Old School theology.

There developed simultaneously another school of theology in the German Reformed Church. It was nurtured in the Mercersburg (Pennsylvania) Theological Seminary; its principal proponent was John W. Nevin (1803-1886), who had been called to the seminary in 1840. He and his associates stressed the centrality of the person of Christ in salvation and his mystical presence in the Lord's Supper. All believers are members of Christ and constitute a mystical body with him. This body is the holy, catholic church which remains one through all the centuries although the character of its life and dogma may be altered. The Mercersburg theologians also called for a return to a higher view of the sacraments and the liturgy, and for this were accused of Romanizing tendencies. With their sense of high churchmanship and mystical sacramentarianism, they constituted the Reformed counterpart to the Neo-Lutheran Movement in Germany and the Oxford Movement in England.

Prior to the opening decades of the nineteenth century American Episcopalianism was dominated by the low-church party, which emphasized the Protestant factor in the church and stressed the authority of the Bible, salvation by faith alone, and the individualistic subjective nature of religion. During the early period, however, the high churchmen also joined in these emphases, but refrained from many cooperative endeavors with Protestants and from participation in humanitarian causes. With the consecration of John Henry Hobart as Assistant Bishop of New York in 1811, the high-church party came into greater prominence.

By the late 1830's, the tension between high churchmen and low churchmen became explosive. Its immediate cause was the Oxford Movement, which was achieving a revival of high churchmanship in England. It was part of a broad reaction against pure rationalism in philosophy and individualism and theological liberalism in religion. It stood for a revival of the catholic character of the Anglican Church. In 1839, Bishop Richard Moore of Virginia, troubled by the significance the Oxford

Movement was acquiring in America, cautioned his convention to guard against "a revival of the worst evils of the Romish system." Two years later Bishop Charles McIlvaine of Ohio, another prominent evangelical, charged the Anglo-Catholic party with rejecting such doctrines as justification by faith and advised them to return to Rome which was their true home.

After 1840, there were signs that even the high churchmen were dividing into two camps. The old high-church party, which centered largely in the East, held to a sacramental conception of the church and emphasized apostolic succession, yet it showed little interest in ceremonialism. The new high-church party, largely an English import which found its greatest influence in the Middle West, was strongly ritualistic. In coming years the high-church position would enjoy a steady gain in influence.

## IMMIGRATION AND RELIGIOUS GROWTH

The threescore and ten years which culminated in the great American Civil War witnessed an eight-fold increase in the country's population. That it rose from nearly 4,000,000 to more than 31,000,000 in a relatively short interval was due partially to a high rate of birth and a reduced death rate, but above all it could be attributed to a tidal wave of immigration which transformed the character of American society. By 1860, the foreign-born residents in the United States numbered approximately one-eighth of the total population. These newcomers were not readily assimilable in their new environment; they tended to form segregated communities where they could preserve the Old World customs and ideologies. That they constituted a menace to the American way of life seemed perfectly plausible to many who feared that which was different. Immigration was thus shadowed by unusual tensions which on occasion flared openly in acts of violence nurtured in the bosom of rabid bigotry.

The Irish were among the most conspicuous in the mass immigration of the 1830's and 1840's. Disease, famine, and revolutions persuaded almost a million Irishmen to emigrate to America by 1845. That year the potato crop failed, striking a mortal blow to Irish economy. In panic, every Irishman who could muster the necessary funds crowded aboard American and Canadian vessels and fled the country. Between 1841 and 1855, nearly 1,600,000 persons, almost one-fifth of the Irish population, migrated to the United States. More than half settled in New York, Pennsylvania, and Massachusetts.

Hard on the heels of the oppressed Irish came a flood of German immigrants, whose number had reached 1,301,136 prior to the outbreak of the Civil War. In Bavaria and the Rhineland, the peasantry suffered severely from the effects of crop failure and the demands of their land-lords. These circumstances, coupled with the fact of impossible tax bur-dens and enforced military service, led thousands to seek transportation to America. Many Germans of Roman Catholic, Lutheran, Reformed, or Jewish persuasion settled in the coastal cities or in the Middle West.

During the 1850's, about 73,000 persons arrived from Denmark, Sweden, and Norway. The Scandinavian countries also had experienced the rigors of famine and poverty, but there were other factors such as discontent with the established church and compulsory military service. The greater majority came via the St. Lawrence River and the Great Lakes and set-tled in Illinois, Minnesota, and Iowa. They were preponderantly Lu-theran.

As the Roman Catholic population climbed steadily, Protestant leaders who had conceived of the United States as a Protestant nation became more and more concerned. In the decade which followed 1825, at least 5,000 Irish Roman Catholic immigrants entered the country each year. To many Protestants, their progress in Americanization seemed painfully, even designedly slow.

Meanwhile, several Roman Catholic missionary societies had been founded in Europe to promote the church's program among emigrants to America. The Society for Propagating the Faith had been organized at Lyons, France, in 1822; in less than thirty years it raised 9,000,000 francs for missionary work in the United States. Other societies were the Austrian Leopold Foundation and the Bavarian Ludwig Mission, both of which adopted as their special project the conversion of the West to Roman Catholicism. Samuel F. B. Morse, inventor of the telegraph, was fully persuaded that the Austrian society was the agency of a sub-versive plot to overthrow American democracy.

Tension reached the breaking point in 1834 in Massachusetts. A young woman who had been dismissed from the employ of the Ursuline Con-vent at Charlestown began to circulate lurid stories of life in the convent. Public indignation over what later was proved to be a completely untrue account was aggravated by the anti-Roman Catholic preaching of Lyman Beecher and many of his fellow clergy. A hastily formed mob descended upon the convent and burned it to the ground.

While some Protestants stood militantly opposed to Roman Catholi-cism, there were many whose thought on the subject was more liberal. Thus John Leland, a Baptist with Jeffersonian sympathies, wrote in 1836 concerning the Roman Catholics: "Should they by fair persuasion . . . increase their number above all other sects collectively, in that case they must of right have the rule; for no man who has the soul of an American will deny the maxim, that 'the voice of the majority is the voice of the whole.'"

Despite the efforts of some to render Roman Catholicism odious to the rank and file of Americans, the church continued to flourish. By 1850, dioceses had been erected in almost every city of considerable size; ten years later the church, with 3,100,000 adherents, constituted the largest single denomination in the United States. More encouraging to the hierarchy was the decision of the national government in 1848 to open diplomatic relations with the Papal States, which included an extensive territory in central Italy. But involved debate with papal authorities over the maintenance of a Protestant church in Rome, together with reports of increasingly reactionary policies by the pope, gradually soured any enthusiasm Americans might have had for the mission. It was terminated by Congress in 1867.

A telling sign of the church's advance was the First Plenary Council or assemblage of the nation's hierarchy, held at Baltimore in 1852. The council issued twenty-five decrees which dealt with such themes as parochial schools, administration of the church's property, and the standardization of discipline, but it ignored fundamental issues such as slavery. The chief significance of the council was that it voiced the church's recognition that its major problems were no longer purely provincial, but national.

Several decades before the high tide of German immigration transformed the character of American Lutheranism, a serious controversy arose in the church between the confessional party, which demanded rigid adherence to the Augsburg Confession and the other symbolical books of the Lutheran tradition, and the "American Lutheran" party, which favored a modification of the confessions in order to bring the church into conformity with the general religious environment. The latter group was headed by Samuel S. Schmucker (1799-1873), a professor at Gettysburg Seminary. "American Lutheranism," however, was not in harmony with the spirit of the times or the ideologies of a majority of German immigrants and therefore lost much of its influence.

The trend toward confessionalism became more pronounced throughout the 1840's and 1850's as a mass of German immigrants began to arrive in the Middle West. Most of these settlers came via the Mississippi River and landed at St. Louis. The first group, which reached Missouri in 1839, had originated in Saxony and had gained a reputation for fervid pietism coupled with rigid Lutheran orthodoxy. The leadership of this band soon fell to a young pastor, Carl F. W. Walther (1811-1887). By 1845, German immigration had increased to such an extent that efforts were made to form a synod. The organization was effected two years later, in Chicago, where Walther was elected first president of the German Evangelical Lutheran Synod of Missouri, Ohio and other States, popularly known as the Missouri Synod. The new synod placed a high value on education under ecclesiastical auspices and soon established a system of parochial schools, colleges, and seminaries.

Another source of Lutheran confessionalism in America was to be found in the Scandinavian immigration which began toward the middle of the century. The first group of Norwegian Lutherans to arrive in the United States settled in Illinois in 1834. Illinois and Wisconsin soon became the chief centers of Norwegian Lutheranism. By 1853, The Synod of the Norwegian Evangelical Lutheran Church of America was organized.

Swedish Lutherans founded their first church in the United States at Andover, Illinois, in 1850, under the pastoral leadership of Lars Paul Esbjörn, advocate of temperance reform and outspoken critic of church establishments. In 1860, he and several other ministers formed The Scandinavian Evangelical Lutheran Augustana Synod of North America.

Late in the eighteenth century, revolutionary movements opened the way for fuller civil liberties for Jews in western Europe. Many Jews began to imbibe the exhilarating intellectual atmosphere; the effect on synagogue life in both Europe and America was tremendous. At first minor changes were made in worship, among them sermons and prayers in the vernacular and organs and choirs. Then changes in the theological climate were noticeable as certain scholars reacted to Biblical authoritarianism. In 1843, a group of Jewish liberals in Frankfurt-am-Main, Germany, organized the Frankfurt Society of the Friends of Reform; they declared acceptance of "unlimited development in the Mosaic religion" but rejection of the authority of the Talmud and the belief that Messiah should lead the Israelites back to Palestine. This manifesto evoked a storm of dissension within Judaism. After 1848, a conservative reaction set in and many German liberals migrated to America.

In the early nineteenth century, reform movements also appeared in the United States. Isaac Harby, in 1824, founded the Reformed Society of Israelites in Charleston, South Carolina. Portions of the service were in English, sermons were preached by the laity, and the congregation worshipped with heads uncovered. The impulse for reform became stronger after 1836 with the advent of Jewish mass immigration from Germany. Between 1840 and 1860, the Jewish population climbed from about 15,000 to 150,000. The real founder of the Reform movement in America was Isaac Mayer Wise (1819-1900). As spiritual leader of congregations at Albany and Cincinnati, he introduced reforms and even published a modernized prayer book.

Although the Reform movement was relatively successful, it developed not without vigorous opposition. In 1829, Mikveh Israel congregation in Philadelphia called to its ministry Isaac Leeser (1806-1868), who sympathized with Reform Judaism in some respects but was more conservative in many of his views. He preached in English but did not sacrifice his essential orthodoxy. As the century wore on the counterreaction of Mikveh Israel and other conservatively minded congregations to Reform principles became more emphatic and led to permanent cleavages in American Judaism.

## THE EMERGENCE OF RELIGIOUS CULTS

If American religion exhibited any common characteristic during that delightfully naïve though turbulent era which preceded the Civil War, it was that it refused to be average. Where restlessness and dissatisfaction with the status quo were most pronounced there was often a tendency to become identified with indigenous cults and movements which sprang up in fertile soil and offered escape from the stark realities of the work-a-day world to a dream land of perfection. This tendency was magnified by the rising tension over slavery, states rights, and nativism, which gripped the country during the three decades of unrest and upheaval antecedent to sanguinary war.

The frontier in particular was a natural breeding ground for bizarre cults and utopian societies which desired some virgin retreat, unblemished by social iniquity, to which they might repair and build their paradise. Rural areas in New England, Pennsylvania, and the Middle West received a goodly representation of dissident groups, but it was in central and western New York that eccentric opinion and unconventional behavior reached their height. From the time of settlement the region was characterized by unusual deviations from doctrinal orthodoxy, clerical exhibitionism, egregious conduct, and frequent change of denominational affiliation. The extravagant emotionalism which accompanied the revivals held in that area gave rise to claims of prophetic gifts and infallible revelations from God, most of which were well received by a superstitious and credulous people.

Central-western New York was the birthplace of Mormonism. Joseph Smith (1805-1844), its founder, had been brought to Palmyra in 1816 by his destitute family which had emigrated from Vermont. One day in 1820, he reported a vision which culminated in his conversion. Later he professed to have been visited by the angel Moroni who told him of a hidden book written on gold plates which gave an account of the former inhabitants of North America. But it was not until 1827 that he was permitted to remove the plates from the hill in which they were buried and translate them. Smith alone saw the plates, which according to his testimony, were written in "Egyptian, Chaldiac, Assyric, and Arabic" characters. The *Book of Mormon* was published in 1830. It treats of the strife between the Nephites, God's chosen people, and the Lamanites or American Indians. By 384 A.D., only a few Nephites, among them Mormon and his son Moroni, were left. Moroni deposited the records of his people for safekeeping in a hill in western New York until a true prophet should arise to disinter them. Actually, there is no part of the work which could not have grown out of Smith's own experience. Where it departs from Biblical thought and style, it reflects the cultural, political, economic, and social ideas of his contemporaries.

In 1830, six persons organized the Church of Jesus Christ of Latter-day Saints, at Fayette, New York. The following year the group moved to Kirtland, Ohio, where they set up a communistic type of community, erected their first temple, and founded a bank. When the bank failed during the Panic of 1837, the Mormons departed for Missouri where they settled temporarily in Caldwell County. From 1840 to 1846, they made their home at Nauvoo, Illinois. Matters proceeded auspiciously until Smith announced that he had received divine authorization to practice polygamy. The incensed non-Mormon people attacked the Mormons and Smith and his brother were taken to jail. On June 27, 1844, an enraged mob descended upon the jail and shot the brothers in cold blood. The majority of Mormons then took as their leader Brigham Young (1801-1877), a convert from Methodism. It was he who led the group in its great trek to the West; by 1847, they had reached the Great Salt Lake. There Young proved himself to be an able and efficient administrator who directed a highly successful cooperative community.

The half century which followed the ratification of the Constitution witnessed the rise of a number of communal sects dedicated to the establishment of an ideal order along religious lines. Almost all the sects interpreted the Bible literally and were pietistic in their emphases. Most believed that by the collective ownership of property they could best prepare themselves for the creation of a perfect order when Christ came again on earth.

One of the earlier communal movements was that of the Shakers, brought from England to America in 1787 by Ann Lee, who claimed to be the recipient of heavenly visions. After the Second Awakening, the movement prospered in the frontier states of Ohio, Kentucky, and Indiana. The Shakers won notoriety for extremes by advocating celibacy and by exalting Ann Lee as the person through whom the Christ Spirit was exhibited a second time. Gradually the sect lost its religious character and by the end of the nineteenth century it was almost extinct.

Among the several experiments in Christian socialism, the Hopedale Community near Milford, Massachusetts, was one of the most prominent. It was founded by a Universalist minister, Adin Ballou (1803-1890), who about 1840 became convinced that it was the duty of Christ's disciples to work for the consummation of the kingdom of heaven on earth. To that end he invited like-minded persons to join him in the formation of an ideal community. Within a year some thirty individuals had adopted a constitution for "Fraternal Communism." As an expression of the movement of social reform which was then sweeping the country, Hopedale sought to banish intemperance, profanity, slavery, capital punishment, war, and all acts known to be in violation of God's will. Then, after a decade of relatively successful community living, the desire for economic gain gradually forged ahead of the dream of a utopian order; in 1856, the community was dissolved and its members went their several ways.

The late 1830's and 1840's witnessed a renewed emphasis upon premillennialism in the American revivalistic sects. This doctrine taught that the earth was in a steady process of moral deterioration and that Christ would soon come again to reign for a thousand years of peace. Since the teaching was most popular in time of trouble, it is understandable that its prestige should have been magnified during the period of economic stress which followed the Panic of 1837.

A leading exponent of premillennialism was William Miller (1782-1849), a Baptist preacher. In 1838, he published lectures in which he predicted the second coming of Christ would take place about the year 1843. The work soon received nationwide publicity and numerous disciples appeared to lend support to the movement. During the summers of 1842 and 1843, more than 100 camp meetings were held in the United States to prepare the people for the advent of Christ. With the dawning of that keenly anticipated year, the tension mounted, for the second coming was expected to occur between March 1843 and March 1844. As the year waxed and waned, expectancy was turned into disappointment, and with the passing of the spring equinox in 1844, a gray pall of gloom settled over the Millerites.

Some of Miller's associates made a further study which prompted them to set another date, October 22, 1844. As the day approached, hundreds of believers congregated in churches and homes to await the coming of Christ. But the day passed into history without the momentous event, and great was the despondency among the faithful throughout the land. A majority of the Adventists returned to their parent churches, though some were permanently lost to the church. Others formed organizations which stressed the premillennialist view. As early as 1844, a small group in Washington, New Hampshire, had begun to observe the seventh-day Sabbath. From this body sprang the Seventh-day Adventists, who developed a denominational organization in 1860.

Excitement over the Millerite movement had scarcely subsided before the cult of Spiritualism appeared on the American scene. The thought of making contact with departed spirits held wide appeal for persons of varied background and character, and nowhere was this more true than in western New York. In March 1848, the family of John D. Fox was disturbed by strange nocturnal rappings in their home at Hydesville, not far from Palmyra, New York. Fox's daughters claimed that the rappings were caused by spirits and devised a system of communication with them. It was not long before the sisters were conducting public seances. Though an investigating committee later discovered that the girls produced the rapping sounds with their toe joints, this in no wise diminished the faith of the general public. Professional mediums throughout the country did a lucrative business through the holding of seances which featured not only rappings but the appearance of unexplained writings and the moving of tables as if by magic. Interest ran high during the 1850's; but with the outbreak of the Civil War, it quickly subsided. Not until the latter part of the century did the movement achieve a national organization.

# CHAPTER NINE

# Social Reform

# in an Age of Conflict

From his vantage point at the middle of the nineteenth century, the historian Emerson Davis reflected thus on the half century which had just elapsed: "There has been . . . a more perfect development of the benevolent spirit of the gospel in the world of men than has been known at any previous time since the age of the apostles." If the statement was somewhat hyperbolic, it was nonetheless expressive of the prevailing ethos in this time of uncritical idealism. The national impulse to achieve a perfect society characterized by benevolence and good will was inspired primarily by that wave of revivals which began with the Second Awakening and mounted with increasing intensity after the opening of the Finney revivals in 1826.

## Ante-Bellum Evangelism

Charles Grandison Finney (1792-1875) united within his person the clerical and scholarly patterns of New England with the lay and pietistic emphases of the frontier. He was the greatest evangelist of the ante-bellum era, first in a line of professional revivalists. Raised in Oneida County, New York, he typified the restless and religiously capricious spirit of that region. It was not until he approached his thirtieth birthday that he had an intense emotional experience which culminated in his conversion to Christianity. Through independent study, he prepared himself for the Presbyterian ministry, but after twelve years of service in that denomination, he withdrew and adopted Congregationalism.

Finney was so successful in winning converts during the opening of his revival campaigns in 1826 that he soon became a peripatetic evangelist, conducting revivals in Philadelphia, New York, and Boston. Wherever he went, congregations were held spellbound by his searching hypnotic eyes and his stentorian voice, which he employed with theatrical effect. Fearful of ostentation, he spoke extemporaneously with straightforward conviction to the common man and yet with such logic that the educated were awed by his homilies. It would be difficult to estimate the number of persons influenced by his ministry; conservatively, it ran into the tens of thousands.

Immediately following the economic collapse of 1837, revivalism entered a lean period, a situation which did not improve during the Mexican War. The evangelist was accepted as a permanent fixture on the national scene, but there were temporarily fewer revivals while the attention of the people was fixed upon economic and political matters. It was not until the fall of 1857 that there were obvious signs of stirrings in the spiritual realm, the first being weekly meetings of laymen for prayer in New York City. About the same time the stock market crash brought on mass hysteria and a popular feeling that the crisis was a divine judgment on a sinful order. The hour had come for national repentance. Thus began a revival distinguished by its urban character and lay leadership.

By February 1858, multitudes were jamming their way into the daily prayer meetings. Similar meetings soon began in Chicago and Philadelphia and it was not long before every large city had regular gatherings for prayer. Gradually the movement gathered strength in the smaller cities, towns, and rural areas until the nation was caught in the full sweep of revivalism. All in all, the awakening of 1858 was a positive force in the direction of spiritual vitality and moral reform which continued in effect through the dark years of the Civil War.

The revival of 1858 bore powerful indications of the influence of perfectionist doctrines which held that a relative attainment of the Christian goal was possible for believers in this life through God's grace. As early as the 1830's, such teachings had emerged at Oberlin Seminary and in the platforms of the various utopian sects. Another important source of perfectionism was the Methodist doctrine of sanctification. It was grounded in Wesley's teaching that through the reception of Christ's saving love men are gradually empowered to perform the works of God and purify their hearts from sinful impulses.

The decade which followed 1850 witnessed a rising tide of perfectionist preaching in the major Protestant denominations. Few non-Methodists adopted the Wesleyan view, but most churchmen were in substantial agreement on the need for individual holiness. To champions of perfectionism the revival of 1858 seemed to presage the coming conversion of the nations and the establishment on earth of the Kingdom of

God. This conviction increased steadily in American evangelical Protestantism throughout and beyond the Civil War.

## MOVEMENTS OF SOCIAL REFORM

It was natural that where there were revivals there should also be reform; it was the means whereby the Kingdom of God was to be achieved in America. As the nineteenth century progressed, interest in a host of moral and social problems mounted steadily in the American Protestant milieu until social reform became the absorbing passion of Christians who embraced revivalism. But not all Protestants could enter with equal enthusiasm into every phase of social reform. The more Biblically legalistic and theocratic thinkers were apt to place their emphasis upon personal reform as a panacea for social evils. Thus the cause of poverty was laziness, pride, and intemperance; through evangelism and Christian education the disease could be remedied. On the other hand, Christians of perfectionist and millennialist inclinations, as well as liberal Unitarians and Friends, tended to identify themselves with such social causes as the abolition of slavery.

In 1815, David Low Dodge, a New York merchant, and thirty others formed a peace society; shortly thereafter several state societies were born. Then, in 1828, the various state societies unified their programs through the organization of the American Peace Society, which proposed arbitration and an international court as solutions to war. With the opening of the tumultuous 1850's, however, the peace movement in the United States rapidly declined in the face of mounting tension over slavery.

The formation of the American Society for the Promotion of Temperance, in 1826, also reflected the moral concerns of the current wave of revivalism. A sister organization, the United States Temperance Union, came into existence in 1833; three years later it merged with the older society to form the American Temperance Union. A number of the delegates desired to ban only strong drinks and to exempt beer and wine from the general condemnation. But their will did not prevail and prohibitionists came to dominate the scene.

With the birth of the Washington Temperance Society in Baltimore in 1840, the movement entered a new phase. A band of reformed alcoholics pledged themselves to total abstinence and the reclamation of inebriates. Their success was astounding; within three years the movement claimed perhaps 100,000 drunkards. Its best-known leader was John B. Gough, himself a convert from drink, who persuaded thousands to sign temperance pledges.

Meanwhile, the older temperance societies began to urge passage of legislation which would curtail the sale of intoxicants. In 1851, the first state-wide prohibition law was enacted in Maine; within four years every northern legislature with the exception of New Jersey had enacted some form of temperance legislation. But by 1860, the public had lost interest in the cause and by 1868 Maine alone had prohibition legislation still in effect.

Concern over the decline of strict Sabbath observance, especially on the frontier, led to the formation of the American and Foreign Sabbath Union in 1843. The reports of Justin Edwards, during his seven-year tenure as secretary, mention that the transportation of mails on the Sabbath had been discontinued on a number of routes and that about forty railroads had terminated train service on that day. In the long run, however, the Sabbath crusaders were doomed to failure. A mighty force against them was the "Continental Sabbath," observed by a majority of European immigrants, which provided for worship on Sunday mornings and for amusement in the afternoons and evenings.

With the steady rise of immigration, the increasing centralization of the population in urban areas, and the uncertainties of employment in an emergent industrial economy, the problem of the poor became more acute. As seen through Puritan eyes, the condition was the result of moral depravity and could be corrected through conversion. But after the devastating effects of the Panic of 1837, certain evangelists began to realize that a new approach was needed to the problem of urban poverty. Edward Norris Kirk suggested in 1842 that "when men love their neighbors as themselves, the causes of poverty will be sought out, and the remedy applied as far as possible." In 1851, Stephen Colwell, Presbyterian layman, took to task the older program of organized benevolence and advocated the passage of social legislation for the protection of the working man.

In this age of evangelical compassion there was born an organization committed to the spiritual development of young men. The Young Men's Christian Association had been founded by George Williams in London in 1844. The first association in the United States was founded in 1851 in Boston; by 1861, there were 200 throughout the country. Their chief activities included conducting prayer meetings, Bible classes, and mission schools, offering lecture courses, and maintaining libraries and reading rooms.

One popular outlet for the expression of humanitarian zeal was prison reform. Its motivation was the moral renovation of the prisoner and the salvation of his soul. At Philadelphia's new penitentiary, erected in 1829, prisoners were isolated and encouraged to read and meditate upon the Bible. The institution at Auburn, New York, was based upon the philosophy that inmates could best rehabilitate themselves through communal labor.

Despite considerable opposition from most of the clergy, women entered more freely into church activities as the nineteenth century progressed and thus contributed to the broader movement which called for equal rights for women in other fields. They participated freely in Bible, tractarian, and Sunday School work and poured themselves into the ministry of poor relief, penal, and antislavery societies. Regarded by men as socially inferior, it was only through persistence that they found a place in the movement for reform. Much of their support came from Quakers, Transcendentalists, and perfectionists who consistently supported democratic ideals and principles.

During the thirty-five years which preceded the Civil War, singular changes were wrought in the character of American Protestantism. Most obvious was the increased function of the laity in the program of the churches, whether through participation in prayer meetings or leadership in humanitarian causes. Since the emphasis among laymen fell upon conversion and the practice of righteousness, there was understandably less concern on their part for denominational differences and the finer points of doctrine. Orthodoxy did what it could to halt the trend, but its seed fell upon rocky ground. The pattern had been set for the development of a liberal and socially centered faith during the remainder of the nineteenth century.

## THE CHURCHES AND THE SLAVERY CONTROVERSY

The post-revolutionary popularization of Deism, the natural rights philosophy, and humanitarianism had profound implications for the slavery issue. They exercised such an effect on public opinion that by 1787 Rhode Island, Vermont, Massachusetts, Connecticut, New York, New Jersey, and Pennsylvania had either abolished slavery or provided for its gradual abolition. In the South several states either prohibited the further importation of slaves or placed restrictions upon their importation. The Congress provided for the abolition of the slave trade in 1808.

While there was a conviction among many of the Protestant clergy that slavery was a social and moral evil, it did not include the reception of the Negro into American society on equal footing with the white. They were convinced that after emancipation the Negro would continue to represent a despised and rejected racial minority and that his presence would upset the social equilibrium of the nation. The answer for many seemed to lie in the return of the Negro to Africa.

By 1815, the number of free Negroes living in America had climbed to the neighborhood of 200,000; approximately half were located in the border states of Delaware, Maryland, Virginia, and North Carolina. For the purpose of transporting these free Negroes to Africa and helping them to build a new life, a group of clergymen and laymen from the Middle Atlantic states organized the American Colonization Society in 1817. Within the first half decade of the society's history it was endorsed by the Presbyterian, Baptist, Methodist, and Episcopal denominations.

It was not long before the society was able to put into effect a program for the founding of Liberia. The first emigrant ship, carrying eighty-nine Negroes, arrived at Sierra Leone in 1821. The enterprise was supported by grants from the national government and from certain states as well as by private philanthropy. During the 1820's, it found favor not only among future abolitionists such as William Lloyd Garrison but among southern slaveholders such as Henry Clay. Many supported it because they believed it would afford an entree to the conversion of Africa. Others thought that it would relieve a heightening social problem, check the rapid rise of the Negro population, and restore unity to the nation.

By 1830, the society was encountering insuperable difficulties. Poverty and disease in Liberia had soured Negro colonists on the venture, while northern philanthropists had discovered that the financial burden was greater than the benefits and that southern slaveholders were not so much interested in emancipation as in ridding their communities of free Negroes. The society's effort to maintain a middle-of-the-road position had only fostered dissension; the South thought it was abolitionist and the North thought it was not abolitionist enough. Thus with the 1830's the society began to decline in importance and the slavery issue became essentially a concern of abolitionists and advocates of slavery.

In view of the changes in the economic situation in the South from 1790 to 1830, it seems not at all surprising that any voluntary program of emancipation was doomed to failure. Slavery, which had appeared to be a gradually dying institution around the end of the eighteenth century because of its relative unprofitability, suddenly took on new value with the invention of Whitney's cotton gin in 1792 and the development of a cotton market in England. Cotton became the main staple produced in the Lower South, and plantation agriculture once again became profitable. Since slaves were indispensable in such an economy, any thought of emancipation was quickly forgotten. By 1860, the number of slaves had risen to nearly 4,000,000.

A young Massachusetts printer, William Lloyd Garrison (1805-1879), launched a vigorous campaign for the immediate release of the slaves with the issuance of his famous *Liberator* in 1831. The following year his associates organized the New England Anti-Slavery Society. In 1833, the movement became national with the birth of the American Anti-Slavery Society, which announced as its purpose the conversion of all Americans to the philosophy that "Slaveholding is a heinous crime in the sight of God" and should at once be abandoned. Soon antislavery societies appeared throughout the North and Middle West. Gradually the movement spread to the churches, several of which organized their own antislavery societies.

By the mid 1830's, a reaction to abolitionism in the North was in full progress. Northern moderates who had worked for colonization deplored the campaign for immediate abolition as a threat to peace. Charles Hodge, Princeton theologian, spoke for this group when he argued that abolitionism would foster antagonism among southerners and promote dissension among those in the North who were sympathetic to the Negro's cause. He did not find slavery condemned in the Scriptures, nor could he discover any evidence that Christ or the apostles had called for its abolition. Nevertheless, he hoped that, through the gradual improvement of the Negro, slavery would be brought to an end.

As the abolitionists continued their aggressive polemics, verbal counterattacks were followed by physical force, prompted by businessmen who feared a loss of trade with the South and workingmen who were concerned over the possible economic competition of free Negroes. Mobs in the North and Middle West broke up meetings of abolitionist societies and threatened their leaders. In Alton, Illinois, the abolitionist editor, Elijah P. Lovejoy, was murdered by a band of fanatics in 1837.

At the opening of the 1840's, Protestants in the North were divided into three groups regarding the question of slavery. On the far left were the decided minority of immediate abolitionists who were willing to sacrifice the Union for the sake of Negro freedom. On the far right were the conservatives who conjured up all sorts of justifications for slavery in order to preserve peace and the Union. In the middle was the party of evangelicals who wished to show love to slaveholders but did not feel they could neglect their antislavery sentiments. As the decade progressed many of these persons, recognizing the increasing determination of the southern proslavery defense and the indecisiveness of their own position, began to lean more toward abolitionism. This tendency was furthered with the passage, in 1850, of the Fugitive Slave Act, which required citizens to cooperate with the authorities in apprehending runaway slaves and returning them to their owners. Antislavery agitation in the North mounted steadily after Harriet Beecher Stowe, in 1852, touched the hearts of the public through the pathos and emotion of *Uncle Tom's Cabin*.

The famous Dred Scott decision of the Supreme Court in 1857, in which the Court ruled that a Negro slave held by his master in free territory was not entitled to freedom, raised a furor throughout the North. Moderate evangelicals were convinced that the time for charity and patience was over. Thus those who for so long had been opponents of radicalism now stood in the camp of immediate abolitionism. They came not to bring peace but a sword with which to amputate the gangrenous member of American society and purify the nation for its divine mission to the world.

It was not until southerners discovered that slavery was economically advantageous that they gave any real attention to its defense on moral and religious grounds. The most significant work of a southerner on the slavery question was by Thomas R. Dew, professor at William and Mary College. In his *Essay on Slavery* (1832), he maintained that slavery was as old as the human race and had been held in honor even among the Jews. It marked "some benevolent design" and was "intended by our Creator for some useful purpose." It tended to reduce the number of wars by introducing ignorant natives to cultured society, in which they might be trained for productive labor and fitted to enjoy a higher standard of living than they could have attained in their former habitat.

Much of the moral justification of slavery originated with the southern clergy, who examined the institution in the light of Biblical teaching. From the Old Testament was drawn the argument that God had decreed slavery and had sanctioned it among the Jews since the time of the patriarchs. From the New Testament was drawn the argument that since Christ had come to fulfill rather than to destroy the law, the institutions of his time did not stand under condemnation. Nor did the apostles teach anything other than the proper submission of a slave to his master.

When clergymen in the North countered with the objection that the proslavery argument was based upon literalism rather than upon the spirit of the Bible, the leading Old School Presbyterian minister in the South, James Henley Thornwell, replied that what they advocated against literalism was rationalism and that nothing could stand more in opposition to the plain teaching of Scripture. That the argument failed to impress northern abolitionists was not surprising; what was important was that it solidified the differences between the opposing parties. In so doing, it too helped to prepare the way for schism and holocaust.

## DENOMINATIONAL SCHISMS

In an age which was not averse to schism it was improbable that abolitionists and slaveholders could long remain within the same denominational camp. The very confidence of each in the righteousness of his cause militated against it. For a few anxious decades both sides struggled valiantly to preserve an uneasy peace; eventually, however, the tensions became too great and the largest Protestant denominations were torn by schism.

The Methodist Episcopal Church was among the first to be rent asunder. During the 1830's, a majority of its officials favored moderate views as a means of preserving unity and were willing to join forces with proslavery southerners to restrain the heavy-handed dealing of northern radicals. In 1842, a group of dissatisfied Methodist abolitionists in New York State seceded from the church, largely because of its refusal to bar slave-holders from its membership, and established the Wesleyan Connection. Moderates in the Methodist Episcopal Church now began to recognize that the price of northern-southern union was northern division. Many decided to take a more favorable look at abolitionism. By 1844, the anti-slavery party in the General Conference had gained sufficiently in strength to vote the suspension from office of a southern slaveholding bishop.

With dispatch the southern proslavery delegates prepared for secession. Bishop William Capers of South Carolina proposed the organization of two General Conferences, one having jurisdiction over Methodists in the slave states, the other administering Methodism in the free states. Finally the General Conference adopted a Plan of Separation, which provided for the equitable distribution of property and the right of ministers to choose between the two denominations. In 1845, delegates from thirteen southern conferences met at Louisville, Kentucky, and organized the Methodist Episcopal Church, South.

Until 1840, when the American Baptist Anti-Slavery Convention met in New York, there was relative peace among northern and southern Baptists. But fear that radical abolitionists might gain control of the missionary societies prompted Alabama Baptists to withhold funds from these agencies until they could be assured that they were free of aboli-tionist influence. The officers of the Triennial Convention, which admin-istered the missionary activities of northern and southern Baptists alike, replied that there was no need for concern inasmuch as they had no right to take any action in regard to slavery. Nevertheless, when the Georgia Baptist Convention proposed the appointment of a slaveholder as a missionary to the Cherokees, the Board of the Home Mission Society vetoed the proposal. Another case brought before the Foreign Mission Board was answered in the same way. It was obvious that abolitionist influence was having a marked effect on both boards.

Without further ado the southern state conventions and auxiliary foreign missionary societies seceded from the national body; at a conven-tion held at Augusta, Georgia, in 1845, the southerners organized the Southern Baptist Convention. Almost no spirit of bitterness pervaded the assemblage; their action was motivated by the sincere conviction that northern and southern Baptists could work best through separation.

New School Presbyterianism, though somewhat more inclined than the Old School toward abolitionism, labored conscientiously to preserve denominational unity through avoidance of an official stand on the question of slavery. Gradually, however, the New School General Assembly became more stringent in its condemnation of slavery, pressured as it was by increasing abolitionist sentiment both in New England and the Middle West. The Assembly of 1857, after protracted debate, adopted resolutions exhorting the membership to repudiate the doctrine that slavery is "an ordinance of God." Indignant over this action, the southern commissioners withdrew and a call went out to the southern churches to form a General Assembly. Thus was born the United Synod of the Presbyterian Church.

Old School Presbyterians, with one-third of their membership in the South, tended to be diplomatic in their dealings with slaveholders while at the same time generally disapproving of slavery. During the critical decade which preceded 1860, a malcontent abolitionist minority was in almost constant conflict with Old School moderates. But the moderates were able to prevent the passage of any inflammatory resolutions on the subject of slavery, thus avoiding schism between the northern and southern wings until the outbreak of war.

That other denominations remained unplagued by schisms over slavery was due to several factors. In the case of Congregationalists and Unitarians it can be explained partially by the fact that their membership was largely in the antislavery North. The Friends, both in the South and North, were very largely opposed to slavery and therefore had no reason to divide. In the Episcopal Church no definite action was taken on slavery. Lutherans made a sharp separation between the sacred and the secular and refrained from involvement in a political matter, while the Disciples of Christ eschewed social reform in favor of personal evangelization. The Roman Catholic hierarchy was unfavorably disposed toward slavery, but believed that its termination should be gradual and according to due process of law. The only schism these churches experienced, therefore, was the political separation necessitated by war. When the conflict drew to its close, their reunion was natural and spontaneous.

## THE CHURCHES AND THE CIVIL WAR

Few wars in modern history have received such overwhelming approval from religious institutions as the Civil War. In both North and South the churches supported their respective governments and made available full spiritual resources for the waging of a conflict which they believed to be under divine control.

Organized Christianity in the North greeted President Lincoln's call for defenders of the Union with enthusiasm; ministers preached their young men into the army and fervently prayed that God might bless the Yankee cause. The General Congregational Association of Connecticut expressed the sentiments of most northern denominations when it called upon all citizens to do everything in their power to suppress "this wicked rebellion" and banish the system of slavery from the land. Similarly, most of the major denominations in the South issued statements of allegiance to the Confederacy at the outset of hostilities. It was fitting that the churches should have backed the government with enthusiasm inasmuch as they had admittedly been in large measure responsible for the secession.

The soldier in the field did not want for attention in the area of religion. The United States War Department, recognizing the need of ministering to the spiritual life of its personnel, authorized the appointment of regularly ordained ministers as chaplains. The various denominations cooperated wholeheartedly in supplying chaplains, of whom the Methodist churches provided about 500. It was not uncommon for a chaplain to organize a regimental church or to conduct protracted revival meetings should the men be kept long in camp. One chaplain of an Indiana regiment won forty-eight persons to the regimental church after a revival. Chaplains performed a variety of services which included counseling homesick or frightened young soldiers, writing to their families, comforting the sick, and burying the dead.

Several charitable institutions were founded for the benefit of the northern soldier. One of the more important was the United States Sanitary Commission, established in 1861. Its principal function was to care for the sick and wounded and for their dependents. Another valuable work was performed by the United States Christian Commission, which grew out of a meeting of Y.M.C.A. delegates in 1861. It distributed among the soldiers books and other reading materials, mostly of a moral and religious nature, and opened libraries and reading rooms in hospitals and camps.

As in the case of the Union army, Confederate military personnel were quite well supplied with chaplains and missionaries who performed similar duties. Many of the South's leading clergymen made regular visits to the troops, notably those in the West, and conducted revivals among them. Perhaps no military organization in history fought with greater assurance that God was on its side than did the Confederate armies. The most hardened veterans appeared regularly at church services and revival meetings and participated in prayer meetings which were often conducted by itinerant ministers and circuit riders. One of Mr. Lincoln's informants was concerned that the southern soldiers were "praying with a great deal more earnestness" than the Union troops.

Those northern Christians of perfectionist and humanitarian inclination who had agitated for the immediate emancipation of the Negro were naturally disappointed when, at the opening of the war, the government took no prompt action to secure his freedom. Nevertheless, the government did take steps toward the abolition of slavery. In April 1862, the Congress provided for the manumission of the 3,000 slaves in the District of Columbia and for the compensation of their former owners. After long and serious reflection, President Lincoln released a preliminary proclamation on September 22, in which he pronounced all slaves living in territories disloyal to the United States to be free as of January 1, 1863. When New Year's Day arrived, the president issued the final Emancipation Proclamation. It was not until the Thirteenth Amendment went into effect in December 1865, however, that slavery was abolished in all states and territories of the United States.

Each legal step toward emancipation was greeted with increasing approval by northern liberals, whether within or outside the church. Antiabolitionists, on the other hand, viewed the process as ruinous to northern unity and dangerous to the well-being of society; the result would be the introduction into the social order of a people culturally unprepared to live as equals with the whites.

As the war progressed and Union troops penetrated deeper into southern territory, large numbers of slaves deserted to their lines and many enlisted in the army. Concern for the education of these people led to the founding of philanthropic organizations such as the American Missionary Association, which, in turn, founded schools for Negroes and staffed them with teachers.

Denominational associations also carried on work among the Negroes. By 1862, the American Baptist Home Mission Society was conducting a program of education for freedmen in the District of Columbia and certain southern states. Most of the Protestant denominations in the North either organized their own Freedmen's societies or contributed to local Freedmen's Relief Associations which were begun during the winter of 1861-1862.

The natural concomitants of war are demoralization and spiritual decline, and the War Between the States was no exception. Urban centers in particular suffered from the chaotic upheaval which accompanied the preparation for and the waging of hostilities. In many cases the churches were weakened by the diversion of their interest and energies to the temporal and the mundane. As the pursuit of spirituality was placed in the background, it became more difficult to sustain Christian institutions and generally there was a decrease in church membership.

There were, however, compensations. If the public in the North was less attracted to the ordinances of formal religion than in normal times, its proclivity for charitable enterprises increased. Not only did people give generously to enterprises conducted for the benefit of the soldiers; they gave freely to the work of home and foreign missions. There was also a marked deepening of tone in the public addresses of the period, indicating a fuller awareness of the sovereignty of God as supreme governor of the nations. The conflict itself was regarded as a mighty work of the Lord for the chastisement and purification of a sinful society.

Toward the end of the war a renewal of interest in religion was evidenced throughout the United States. Church periodicals reported a growing wave of revivalism which bore fruit in a gradual increase in church membership and a heightened sense of Christian responsibility. The return to religion, however, was not sufficiently dynamic to ward off the evil influences which accompanied the war. Intemperance had once again become a major problem for society, while selfishness and greed brought a moral desolation which would grip the nation for decades to come.

In the South, the churches continued as the chief builders of morals throughout the war. From the pulpits was sounded a call to crusade for righteousness and an invocation for divine assistance. It was not uncommon for churches to conduct daily prayer meetings. The government also arranged for days of thanksgiving and for times of fasting and prayer. In the face of increasing adversity and military setbacks, thousands of persons hoped that the spiritual power released by manifold fervent prayers might lead to improved conditions.

There was, nevertheless, a strong element of secularism running through southern society which was heightened by the distractions of war. As in the North, the presence of moral laxity and religious indifference as growing perils in the Confederacy were all too evident. As the dark hours of defeat were superseded by the black years of Reconstruction, a sense of futility and despair beclouded the once serene countenance of a romantic and gallant South. The carefree days of southern adolescence were over; ahead lay the grim shadows of poverty and social turmoil as an embittered and chastized people struggled for redemption.

CHAPTER TEN

# Church Extension

# and Consolidation

As the cruel war between the Blue and the Gray came to a grinding halt at Appomattox, in every section of the nation enormous energies were released in personal and social aggrandizement. White southerners, trampled under the heavy boot of Reconstruction, struggled valiantly to regain status in government and to avoid economic catastrophe; their former slaves, dazzled by the splendiferous glare of freedom, seized every opportunity to find position and prestige in a time of rapid social transition. In the North the phenomenal development of machine-industry and the accelerated rise of great urban centers testified to the kaleidoscopic changes which were taking place in American life. Beyond the broad Missouri, armies of intrepid adventurers hastened westward to conquer the last frontier.

## THE CHURCHES AND RECONSTRUCTION

After the fall elections of 1866, the Radical Republicans, determined to work their vengeance on a hated South, were clearly in the majority in both houses of the Congress; the result was that the South was placed under the control of five military districts. Thus began the chaotic period of rule by northern Carpetbaggers, turncoat Scalawags from the South, and misguided Negroes who were swept into positions for which they had no preparation. Not until 1877 were the last Federal occupation forces withdrawn from the South.

It was the sincere conviction of northern church members that the southern churches had become so depraved that only with the help of northern missionaries was there any hope of their being cleansed. With a deep assurance of the righteousness of their cause, these missionaries moved into the South to convert the "apostates." Southern church-men, however, did not regard themselves as fit subjects for conversion and greeted the invaders with bitter invective and scorn. Without the presence of Federal bayonets, the position of the northern missionaries would have been untenable indeed. Actually the northern churches tended to lose interest in converting white southerners after the first blush of Recon-struction fervor and settled down to the work of educating the Negro.

The principal concern of organized religion during the era of Recon-struction was the education and social advancement of the freedman. Through sudden political upheaval he had been thrust into a society which granted him a liberty for which he had not been adequately prepared; without the paternalistic guidance of white masters, a life of freedom often produced more bewilderment than confidence. It was the northern churches more than any other group of institutions that took the freedman in hand and ministered to his economic, intellectual, moral, and spiritual needs.

One of the more important organizations which carried education to the Negro was the American Missionary Association, a nondenom-inational society supported mainly by Congregationalists. It offered schooling from the elementary grades through college and maintained theological seminaries to train Negro ministers. The greater proportion of Negro college graduates during the first half century after emancipa-tion found their way into the ministry or teaching.

Of the 4,441,830 Negroes in the United States in 1860, perhaps 520,000 or 11.7 per cent were church members. During and after the war, the trend among Negroes was to withdraw from the white denominations and unite with existing Negro communions or form new denominational structures. In 1863, the African Methodist Episcopal Church initiated work in Virginia, while the African Methodist Episcopal Zion Church inaugurated missionary programs in North Carolina and Louisiana. After the termination of hostilities, both communions developed rapidly in the South, partially through the transfer of members from the Methodist Episcopal Church, South. During the period of Reconstruction, this latter body lost more than half of its colored membership. Among colored Baptists there was a similar withdrawal from the white churches and the formation of new denominational bodies. The democratic organization of the Baptist churches together with the popular appeal of baptism by immersion were powerful factors in winning Negroes to that persuasion and help to account for the fact that in the post-war era Baptists came to surpass Methodists in numerical strength.

American Negroes developed no new denominational types of major significance. They preferred to follow those basic structures with which they had become familiar during their period of slavery, leaning heavily on Baptist and Methodist doctrine and polity. Their general conformity to the religious practices of the whites was evident in their services of worship and in the organization of their churches. The order of worship and the character and function of the sermon were patterned after the standard practice in America, particularly those of the evangelical, low-church variety. Negro churches also adopted such well-accepted institutions as Sunday Schools, youth groups, societies for women, and mid-week prayer meetings. Church-affiliated organizations of this kind not only served the cause of spiritual growth but filled a definite need for a people which enjoyed few if any other outlets for social expression.

## THE CHALLENGE OF THE FRONTIER

A cartographer charting the bounds of the American frontier in 1865 would have drawn a line southward from the western border of Minnesota, making it bulge westward to include portions of Nebraska and Kansas, and terminating it in central Texas. He would have shown that east of this line there was still much unoccupied land and that west of it there were settled districts in the Willamette and Columbia valleys, in the areas near San Francisco and San Diego, and in the Mormon country of Utah. Most of the territory west of the line, however, represented frontier territory inhabited only by Indians and wildlife. Yet by 1890, this vast region would be virtually conquered for white civilization and carved into states and territories.

Burgeoning settlements in the West presented the churches with new challenges and opportunities. In areas such as the mining camps, where men were rough and profane, the ordinances of religion were generally ill-received, and it was not uncommon for missionaries to be run out of town. In the more settled agricultural centers, religion was usually welcomed as a stabilizing influence and chambers of commerce in the new cities supported the establishment of churches. To meet a growing need the denominations organized boards and agencies to inaugurate religious programs in promising areas and to found churches wherever possible. Thus the Methodist Church Extension Society was organized in 1864, the Congregational National Council in 1865, and a number of similar denominational agencies after 1870. During the 1860's, Protestant organizations of this type raised and spent an average of about $2 million per year; by the 1880's, the figure had reached the $4-million mark.

Until 1890, the principal interest of the extension societies was the occupation of new territory and the development of new churches. Basically the churches followed the line of the railroads. Chaplain C. C. McCabe, who served from 1868 to 1884 as assistant secretary of the Methodist Church Extension Society, rode the trains from town to town establishing churches or superintending their erection. To the claim of the prominent freethinker, Robert G. Ingersoll, that the churches were "dying out all over the land," McCabe countered with the boast that the Methodists were building more than one church a day and expected soon to increase the number to two.

In the taming of the American West there emerged certain leaders of outstanding importance who made an imperishable mark upon the new society. Such a leader was the Presbyterian missionary, Sheldon Jackson (1834-1909). At the conclusion of the Civil War, he was appointed "superintendent of missions for Western Iowa, Nebraska, Dakota, Montana, Wyoming, and Utah." A human dynamo, he traveled unceasingly throughout his vast territory of responsibility, planting churches and ministering in countless other ways. It was not long before he extended his missionary activities to Colorado, New Mexico, Arizona, and Nevada. In 1877, he visited Alaska and was so overwhelmed by the educational and spiritual needs of this new frontier that he devoted much of the remainder of his life to its cultivation.

Possibly 225,000 Indians were scattered throughout the West in 1860; the greater majority stayed within their preserves and maintained the peace. With the rapid influx of white settlers after the war and the government's decision to remove the Indians to less desirable lands, there began a period of almost incessant conflict between the natives and the whites which lasted until 1886. When the conflict finally drew to a close, the Indians had been so decisively defeated that they had no choice but to accept a life of dependence on reservations provided by the national government.

Christian missions among the Indians were at best difficult. Since the natives were divided into many tribes which spoke different dialects, no one missionary could expect to reach a great number. The churches, nevertheless, sent hundreds of missionaries to the Indian tribes; these persons not only brought the Gospel to the natives but helped them adjust to a new way of life in a society dominated by white men. By 1914, probably 40 per cent or more of the Indians were nominal Christians or at least subjected to Christian influence. It has been estimated that of the approximately 400,000 Indians living in the United States in 1950, 28 per cent were Protestant, 28 per cent Roman Catholic, and 44 per cent either pagan or uncommitted. In all likelihood this estimate is too generous on the side of Christian commitment.

## THE FLOOD OF IMMIGRATION

By 1880, there were 6,680,000 foreign-born persons living in the United States; among these were about 2,000,000 Germans, 1,855,000 Irish, 717,000 Canadians, 664,000 English, and 440,000 Scandinavians. Assimilation of these people was not difficult inasmuch as they had descended from the same stock as the Anglo-Saxon people. The influx from northern and western Europe, which was greatly encouraged by under-populated states, reached its crest in 1882 and henceforth declined. As the years passed, the multitudes from Russia, Austria-Hungary, Italy, and other countries along the Mediterranean continued to increase until, in 1896, they were arriving in greater numbers than those from northern Europe. There were many reasons for this heavy immigration—overpopulation in the mother country, persecution of Jews in Russia beginning in the 1880's, the inauguration of direct steamship service between Mediterranean and American ports, and the lure of employment in recently opened mines and factories. These later immigrants were inclined to isolate themselves from the rest of society, perpetuating as long as possible their Old World customs and native dialects. During the thirty-five years between 1865 and 1900, no less than 13,500,000 aliens arrived on these shores, a figure surpassing by more than a million the total population in 1830. And this was slight when compared with immigration in the opening decades of the twentieth century.

Gradually popular enthusiasm for immigration began to cool. Organized labor in particular raised its voice in protest against unrestricted immigration which was creating excessive competition for jobs. In 1917, a literacy test was enacted as a prerequisite to admission to the country. The most restrictive legislation, however, was the Immigration Act of 1924, which fixed the quotas at 2 per cent of the foreign-born of each nationality counted in the census of 1890 and excluded all Japanese.

Organized religion bore the obvious marks of the impact made by mass immigration. Some religious bodies experienced an appreciable gain in membership, with other religious expressions appearing for the first time on the American scene. Those bodies most affected by the tidal wave of immigration were the Lutheran, Roman Catholic, Jewish, and Eastern Orthodox.

Between 1870 and 1910, Lutheran church membership in the United States rose from less than 500,000 to almost 2,250,000 so that in numerical strength the Lutheran churches were elevated to third place among Protestant denominations. This gain was made possible largely through heavy German and Scandinavian immigration, notably to the Upper

Mississippi Valley. The greater majority of Scandinavians came from a Lutheran background but were theologically more liberal than many Germans. Once in America, numbers of them departed from their Old World heritage. In some cases this resulted in free-church tendencies within American Lutheranism; in others it led to affiliation with denominations other than the Lutheran or with no church at all.

With the formation of the Augustana Synod in 1860, Scandinavian Lutheranism in America set out in a new direction. The trend in the churches of the Synod was to favor unqualified subscription to the Augsburg Confession, to attach greater importance to the work of the laity, to stress the personal religious experience, and to give a pietistic interpretation to the Christian life. In 1870, the Norwegian element in the Synod, having desired a fellowship which would be dominantly Norwegian, withdrew and promptly divided into two denominational bodies. That same year the Swedish group merged with the theologically conservative General Council of the Evangelical Lutheran Church of North America. One of the larger Norwegian bodies was the Synod for the Norwegian Evangelical Lutheran Church in America, organized in 1853 by persons who favored a strict interpretation of doctrine and rigid adherence to the ritual and procedure of the Norwegian Church.

Possibly the most dynamic of all the Lutheran bodies was the strictly orthodox Missouri Synod. This denomination, which held to the infallible character of the Scriptures and full acceptance of the Lutheran confessions, carried its message with indefatigable zeal to German immigrants during the last half of the nineteenth century and with such success that by 1890 its number of communicants had risen to 293,211.

During the last decades of the nineteenth century, a rather heavy German immigration swelled the ranks of the Roman Catholic Church in America. After 1900, however, the accessions from Italy, Austria-Hungary, and Poland proved to be more important. A large migration of French Canadians into the United States added significantly to Roman Catholic strength in New England and northern New York, while the entrance of more than 100,000 Mexicans into the Southwest by 1900 had the same effect. In June 1908, Pope Pius X declared that the church in America was no longer to be regarded as missionary territory but was now on a par with other great national bodies such as those in France and Italy. By 1900, the church had a membership of 12,000,000 or nearly 16 per cent of the total population.

The church, nevertheless, suffered serious losses through "leakage" to other denominations or the secularization of the immigrant. The greatest losses were incurred in the urban areas which attracted the largest numbers of immigrants, especially in the metropolitan districts of the East. Manifold reasons may account for this situation: an insufficient number of priests to minister to the personal needs of the immigrant, the impersonal nature of parishes in the big cities, preoccupation with economic concerns, and the attractions of secularism. The church made every effort to keep up with the immigrant, establishing dioceses as quickly as growth in population warranted.

A perennial fear of many non-Roman-Catholic Americans was that the church was essentially a foreign power which, if allowed to expand without limitation, would bring to an end the American way of life. This fear was not assuaged by the issuance of the *Syllabus of Errors* (1864) by Pope Pius IX, in which he condemned, among many others, the propositions that Protestantism is an acceptable form of the Christian religion and that church and state should be separated. Many American bishops did everything possible to disabuse the public of the idea that Roman Catholics were un-American; their task was admittedly difficult.

In the realm of doctrine, a rising attitude of devotion to the Virgin Mary had led to the definition of the Immaculate Conception by Pope Pius IX in 1854 as a dogma of the church. It taught that from the moment of her creation Mary had been "immune from all taint of original sin." Devotion to the Virgin increased steadily; and on November 1, 1950, Pope Pius XII proclaimed the bodily assumption to heaven of the Virgin Mary as a dogma to be accepted by all communicants.

Another trend during the pontificate of Pius IX was toward ultramontanism, a view which suggested that the church should look to Rome for its final authority. With the thought that the time was ripe for a definition of papal infallibility, Pius IX summoned a general council of the church to meet at the Vatican late in 1869. Many bishops were reluctant to give their approval to such a definition, thinking it inopportune. The members of the American hierarchy saw that its passage could prove injurious to the church in the United States by fomenting anti-Catholic prejudice. But when the vote was taken in 1870, only two bishops replied in the negative. One of these was Bishop Edward Fitzgerald of Little Rock, Arkansas; and he accepted the doctrine as soon as it was proclaimed. As promulgated by the pope in the document known as *Pastor aeternus,* the doctrine provided that when the pope defines a doctrine regarding faith or morals, he "is possessed of that infallibility with which the divine Redeemer willed that His Church should be endowed for defining doctrine regarding faith or morals: and that therefore such definitions of the Roman Pontiff are irreformable of themselves, and not from the consent of the Church."

Clearly the most distinguished member of the American hierarchy in the fifty-year period following 1870 was James Gibbons (1834-1921), Cardinal Archbishop of Baltimore. Judicious in temperament and broad in sympathy, he sought out men of all classes and persuasions and fraternized with non-Roman Catholics more than any member of the hierarchy ever had before. He wanted a virile and unified Roman Catholicism, thoroughly assimilated into the American environment; his life was dedicated to the achievement of that goal.

Pope Leo XIII allowed some of the opinions of Gibbons to pass without condemnation. By January 1899, however, he had decided to issue the papal letter *Testem benevolentiae,* addressed to Cardinal Gibbons; in it he condemned the kind of Americanism which thought that the church should harmonize itself with modern theories, abrogate its right to determine all questions of a doctrinal and moral character, and permit the individual greater initiative in the development of his spiritual life. The letter was at once clear and final; with its issuance an era of liberalizing tendencies and wide fraternization came to an end.

After 1871, Jewish immigration from Germany declined; thenceforth the bulk of Jewish immigrants came from eastern Europe. Mainly because of Russian persecution, Polish, Roumanian, and Russian Jewish immigration reached tremendous proportions in the 1880's.

During the years immediately following 1865, Reform Judaism took on much of the character of upper-middle-class Protestantism, with most of the distinctively Jewish features removed. Its standards were fixed at a conference assembled in Pittsburgh in 1885. They provided for the rejection of all Mosaic laws concerned with ceremonialism which could not be harmonized with modern civilization. In 1889, Rabbi Isaac Mayer Wise organized a Central Conference of American Rabbis, composed of Reform spiritual leaders.

The solidification of the Reform position prompted a vigorous reaction on the part of conservative leaders. Rabbi Sabato Morais (1823-1897) founded the Jewish Theological Seminary Association in 1885 and began to hold classes in New York. The purpose of the seminary was to train for the rabbinate those Jews who were "faithful to Mosaic Law and ancestral traditions."

Judaism in eastern Europe remained uninfluenced by the Reform movement; within the sphere of religion there was an assiduous adherence to orthodoxy and tradition quite unknown to German Judaism. It was inevitable that, when the eastern European group finally confronted in the United States their Americanized German Reform brethren, feeling should have been intense. But gradually the tension was overcome through an increasing willingness on the part of well-established Jews to help their less fortunate coreligionists and by a growing tendency on the part of the newcomers to adjust to their surroundings and become assimilated into the American environment.

Soon the older, established Conservative element began to draw closer to the east-European Orthodox groups in the hope that their association would be mutually advantageous. Rabbi Henry Pereira Mendes of New York tried to strengthen the position of Conservative Judaism by allying it with Orthodoxy; in 1898, he led in the establishment of the Union of Orthodox Jewish Congregations. This Union soon fell under complete control of the Orthodox and thus proved to be unsatisfactory to the Conservatives.

In the meantime, the Conservative movement enjoyed a period of vitality and growth; and in 1913, Solomon Schecter, president of the Jewish Theological Seminary, gathered sixteen congregations to form the United Synagogue of America. It stood between Orthodoxy and Reform, recognizing the authority of Jewish religious and ritual law and emphasizing the importance of the Hebrew language, but also accepting the findings of historical criticism when demonstrated beyond reasonable doubt.

The same mass movement which brought thousands of Orthodox Jews to the United States was responsible for the arrival of additional thousands of Christians representing the Eastern Orthodox churches. The bulk of these immigrants, which were by no means as many as the Jews, arrived between 1880 and 1920. Their principal purposes in coming were to escape the effects of poverty, revolutions, and wars. While they were one in dogma and practice, taking as their authority the Scriptures, the decrees of the seven ecumenical councils of the ancient church, and the traditions, they were organized for the most part along national lines and therefore looked to different patriarchs for leadership. When the various adherents arrived in the United States, they tended to perpetuate their national alignments.

While Russian Orthodoxy had made some impression on the Pacific Coast and in Alaska prior to the Civil War, it was not until 1876 that a Russian Orthodox church was founded in New York and not until the 1880's and 1890's that any noteworthy immigration of Orthodox Christians to America began. During this period, Russian parishes were established in New York and Chicago. In 1905, the episcopal see in San Francisco was transferred to New York and made an archdiocese.

It was not unil the period between 1890 and 1914 that a substantial immigration from Greece swelled the ranks of the Greek Orthdox Church in the United States. Upon application by the newcomers to the appropriate religious officials, a number of priests were dispatched to this country and soon congregations were organized in the larger cities. No complete church organization was effected, however, until 1918, when Bishop Alexander was sent to America as first bishop and synodical delegate. In 1922, the Patriarchate of Constantinople erected the Greek Archdiocese of North and South America.

Because of barriers raised by the American government, the number of Asiatics in the United States has never been large. The second half of the nineteenth century witnessed the arrival of more than 100,000 Chinese on the West Coast, where they were at first welcomed as inexpensive laborers. Then, when white laborers began to compete with them for jobs, anti-Chinese feeling arose and the result was violence. About the turn of the century there was a sharp increase in Japanese immigration, so that by 1910 there were 72,157 Japanese in the country. Anti-Japanese sentiment also developed, particularly on the West Coast where Japanese were numerous.

Many Protestant leaders viewed the arrival of Asiatics, few of whom were Christian, as a unique missionary opportunity. As early as 1852, William Speer, a Presbyterian missionary who had served in Canton, China, began a mission among the Chinese of San Francisco. By 1870, similar activities had been started by the Baptists, Methodists, and Congregationalists. Despite a vigorous missionary effort, the number of conversions was small; in 1900, probably not more than 2 per cent of the Chinese population had been converted to Christianity. The first mission for the Japanese was founded in 1877 in San Francisco. But the influence of Buddhism remained strong, particularly among the Japanese.

# CHAPTER ELEVEN

# Religious Life
# in the Victorian Era

To the representative American churchgoer during the decades immediately following the Civil War, religion was first and foremost a matter of integrity and respectability. He might be careless in his orthodoxy, slovenly in his worship, and indifferent in his attitude toward social ills; but he was anxious not to be denied a reputation for piety, charity, and unimpeachable conduct. He wore his religion much as he did his Prince Albert coat; it was a thing of pride, a symbol of status pointing to his dignity as a man. In theory he knew himself to be a sinner for this was the pronouncement of orthodoxy, but he never allowed formality to stand in the way of practice. Orthodoxy was his profession; activism was his life. Thus he patronized a multiplicity of causes which crusaded against sin, blissfully neglecting the complex and demonic forces which contributed to public corruption and social upheaval. He supported the church as a cause worthy of his backing and regarded Sunday attendance as much a favor to his pastor as a benefit to his soul.

## TRENDS IN PULPIT AND PEW

The last half of the nineteenth century witnessed significant changes and trends in the character and position of the American churches. First and most obvious was the phenomenal gain in membership; whereas 16 per cent of the population were church affiliates in 1850, 36 per cent were so related in 1900. Everywhere there were signs of prosperity and expansion in the churches. Where once there was a simple frame meetinghouse there stood now a majestic edifice of brick or stone, testifying to the affluence of its congregation. Robed choirs, strengthened by professional singers, marched with dignity to their stations in the chancel, accompanied by the swelling chords of great organs; and ministers, increasingly conscious of worship as a fine art, devoted more attention to conducting their services "decently and in order."

The growing interest in liturgics late in the nineteenth century in no wise detracted from the glory of the American pulpit. It was the age of homiletical oratory, when knights of the pulpit could hold thousands enthralled as they fought all manner of evil with the sharp sword of rhetoric. To many congregations the portions of the service preceding the sermon were still the "preliminaries"; their purpose was to lead the worshipper to the climax of the service, the sermon. In the large cities congregations vied with one another for the distinction of having the most popular and sensational preacher. To be able to hold an audience spellbound became a standard criterion of ministerial success.

Few American clergymen could hope to compete for publicity with the nationally known Henry Ward Beecher (1813-1887), who dominated the pulpit of Plymouth Church, Brooklyn, from 1847 to the end of his life. Through a long pastorate he came to be recognized as the most creative personality and one of the great oratorical geniuses of the American pulpit. He had the happy faculty of being able to present the most advanced thought of his generation in language easily understood by ordinary men and to stamp it indelibly, by means of word pictures, upon their minds.

One of the most unforgettable preachers of all time was the saintly Phillips Brooks (1835-1893). His preaching was not of a type which called attention to itself; it was always straightforward, though poetic, and in its rapid delivery thrust deftly like a rapier into the heart. Called by Trinity Church, Boston, in 1869, he soon became the city's favorite son and his church was regularly packed with persons who went away uplifted by his presence and charmed by the music of his voice.

Possibly the most amazing trend in the Victorian era was the growing influence of laymen in the Protestant denominations. As the churches became larger business enterprises, their physical control fell more and more under the jurisdiction of boards of trustees composed of businessmen. Many denominations invited laymen to accept administrative positions in their national offices, while prominent businessmen frequently served as treasurers of denominational societies. The trend toward administration was felt even by the clergy, who were encouraged to add the function of business executive to their already staggering burdens. Deans, district superintendents, stated clerks, synodical presidents, and bishops found that administrative prowess was considered as essential to effective leadership as education and piety.

## The Upsurge of Revivalism

Since the Great Awakening, revivalism had been established as a permanent feature of American Protestantism. For the most part its effectiveness had depended upon the personal persuasiveness of eminent clergymen. This circumstance changed during the revival of 1857-1858, a spontaneous movement almost free of professional evangelists and directed by laymen. Perhaps its main contribution to future revivals was to train a force of lay evangelists, among them Dwight L. Moody, for subsequent service. Revivalism was temporarily eclipsed by secular and materialistic interests brought on by war, and challenged by the flood tide of immorality and corruption which accompanied and followed the conflict. America, in the post-Civil War era, was ripe for another upsurge of revivalistic zeal. It was not long in coming.

The leading revivalist of the late nineteenth century was Dwight Lyman Moody (1837-1899). As a young and successful shoe salesman in Chicago, he had dedicated his life to personal evangelism and had founded a nondenominational mission Sunday School. After service with the United States Christian Commission during the Civil War, he acted as lay pastor of a church under Congregational auspices. Events moved swiftly after 1871. By this time Moody had joined forces with Ira D. Sankey, a Methodist layman with a gift for religious song. On Moody's third trip to England in 1873, this time with Sankey, he began a two-year revival which won thousands to an acceptance of Christ. In 1875, the two evangelists returned to America in triumph; that October they held their first important series of meetings in Brooklyn and took the city by storm. Philadelphia and New York were next, with equally impressive results. Unlike many earlier revivalists who used hyperemotional techniques to win converts, Moody appealed in a simple and straightforward manner to the reason as well as the emotions. Persons converted at his meetings were shepherded into smaller inquiry rooms where they met with trained workers and were directed to some local church.

In his theology Moody was thoroughly orthodox. He did not, however, place equal emphasis on all teachings of the Scriptures. At the very center of his theological system was God's love, and he preached it as few Christians had preached it before. Yet in his zeal to proclaim the love of God he neglected other aspects of dogma so that many came to believe Moody's simple teaching was the whole Gospel. Thus he contributed to a decline in theological interest and indirectly gave comfort to those forces which were promoting liberalism.

For a full generation after the Moody revivals a series of lesser revivalists, among them Sam Jones, Gypsy Smith, R. A. Torrey, and J. Wilbur Chapman, followed in the steps of the great master. Undoubtedly the most accomplished showman was William (Billy) A. Sunday (1863-1935). Between 1914 and 1919, he conducted numerous revival meetings in the larger cities of America; in New York he claimed 98,000 converts. Sunday was known for his lack of propriety in speech and his pulpit gyrations. On the platform he could be expected to hurl chairs at "the Devil," shake his fists at all manner of sinners, and run and slide across the stage in an impersonation of some reprobate trying to gain heaven by the same means a ball player might try to gain home plate. His message was sincere even though his presentation of the Gospel was somewhat one-sided. He lived in a delightfully naïve world which failed to recognize the complexities of modern life and supposed all ethical decisions afforded easy solutions. By 1920, his age had drawn to a close; the jazz age loomed just ahead.

## Religious Education and Culture

The third quarter of the nineteenth century witnessed an attempt on the part of Sunday School leaders to improve the curriculum. The result was the overthrow of the catechetical method of Bible study and the creation of uniform lessons by the Fifth National Sunday School Convention in 1872. According to this system, each participating school would study the same lesson simultaneously in all classes, thus unifying the work of the school. However, the trend in secular education to place the child at the center of the curriculum and to use the newest approved methods of educational science for his training was soon felt in the demand of the churches for a richer curriculum suited to the needs of the pupils. In 1908, the Twelfth International Sunday School Convention (the movement had become international after 1872) authorized the preparation of a closely graded series of lessons, with separate study materials for each grade or year. After 1914, the Uniform Lessons provided separate helps for the Primary, Junior, Intermediate, Senior and Young People's, and Adult departments.

The closing decades of the century were also marked by a heightened interest in providing special programs of worship, study, and recreation for young people, apart from the formal activities of the Sunday School. To this end, Dr. Francis E. Clark organized the first Christian Endeavor Society at Portland, Maine, in 1881. It was a self-managed society of young people which provided worship and instruction and invited each person to participate in the program. Clark's idea caught the attention of church leaders throughout the country and in other lands, and within six years more than 7,000 societies had been formed with a membership approaching 500,000. Various denominations preferred to develop their own youth organizations, though some allowed their local societies of Christian Endeavor to continue.

A most important new educational device was developed in 1874 when John H. Vincent, minister and later bishop of the Methodist Church, and Lewis Miller, an Ohio manufacturer, organized a two-week summer assembly for training Sunday School teachers, at Lake Chautauqua, New York. It soon blossomed into an all-summer assembly with courses and lectures on various themes. Prominent scholars and preachers from all over the country attracted thousands of eager middle-class adults who sat enthralled at their feet. No institution in American history so effectively blended religion and culture and presented them in such a palatable form.

## MOVEMENTS OF REFORM

American morals in the Victorian period were conspicuous for the wide disparity between the professed attitudes of the nominally religious and respectable and the observed conduct in the social order. Americans might be reluctant to criticize the fastidious principles of the time, but they were somewhat less hesitant to ignore them. After the Civil War there was a deplorable laxity of morals in both private and public life. Business was controlled by railway magnates, steel kings, and coal barons who relentlessly fought for power and amassed huge fortunes at the expense of the public. In the area of politics, corruption was rampant on national, state, and local levels. Many cities were controlled by political machines, the most infamous of which was the "Boss" Tweed ring in New York.

If the majority of American churchmen were indifferent to the financial and political corruption of the era, their concern over worldly amusements was serious to the point of being devastating. To puritan and perfectionist thinkers, it was difficult to conceive of greater moral perils than dancing, attending the theater, gambling, smoking, and drinking; and many vehemently criticized institutions which offered facilities for these pursuits.

The increase of immigration was a social phenomenon which had effects on moral codes as well as upon economic life. In urban centers in particular Protestant Christians were concerned to see the newcomers ignore old-fashioned Sabbath observance in favor of a day of relaxation and amusement. To the strait-laced, the Germans with their "Continental Sunday," the Irish, Italians, and Poles with their Catholic Sunday, and the Jews with their holy day on Saturday, constituted a threat to the American way of life. The epitome of moral degeneration was to spend one's Sunday evening in a German beer garden. Ministers decried the fact that more of the public purchased Sunday newspapers, frequented ball parks and other amusement centers, went on excursions, or simply stayed at home, but they were unsuccessful in halting the trend.

Between 1860 and 1880, the capital investment in the liquor industry climbed from $29 million to $190 million. The rise in liquor consumption was most evident in the cities where saloons became favorite gathering places for workingmen. An effective campaign against liquor was waged by the Women's Christian Temperance Union, the first chapter of which was formed in 1873. During its early years a determined membership organized crusades against the saloons; they would march boldly into the "dens of iniquity," hold prayer meetings for the benefit of patrons, and in some cases persuade the saloonkeeper to pour his product into the gutter. After 1879, the organization devoted much of its energies to agitation for temperance education in the public schools. The W.C.T.U., which had ample support from the churches, became highly influential in shaping public opinion.

The campaign against liquor took on a new vitality with the creation of the Anti-Saloon League of America in 1895. It engineered an intensive drive to organize the anti-liquor interests for political action. The result was that eight southern states had adopted state-wide prohibition by 1915, and by 1916 six western states had taken the same course. In states which did not have state-wide prohibition, the local option movement enjoyed considerable popularity, particularly in rural areas. Finally, in 1919, the Eighteenth Amendment, which prohibited the manufacture, transportation, or sale of intoxicants, became a part of the Constitution. The following year the Volstead Act defined illegal beverages as those containing more than half of one per cent of alcohol.

To a considerable extent the feminist campaign during the late nineteenth century for broader rights in society was linked with the movement for temperance and prohibition, many of its leaders being active in the W.C.T.U. A left wing of the feminist movement was principally concerned with gaining the suffrage and other civil rights, while a more conservative element worked for the formation of women's organizations which advanced culture and encouraged young ladies to attend college. That many women were able to make significant contributions to organized religion was due in large measure to the invaluable training they received in these organizations. Most churches refused to endorse woman suffrage but allowed women to work in church societies. Nevertheless, the patriotic activities of American women during World War I broke down opposition to their receiving the vote, and the Nineteenth Amendment to the Constitution, which prohibited voting restrictions on the basis of sex, was ratified in 1920.

## ORTHODOXY UNDER FIRE

To the uncritical observer the American theological scene at the close of the Civil War appeared to be unruffled by doctrinal dissension. It was not long, however, before orthodoxy in many of the denominations was challenged by a variety of intellectual forces which fostered more liberal concepts. Some communions modified their theological position to provide greater latitude of thought, while others intensified their efforts to preserve the purest orthodoxy. The process was accompanied by impassioned debate and hard-fought heresy trials.

Charles Darwin's *Origin of Species* (1859) made little impact upon the American consciousness, except among scientists, until after the Civil War. Its principal thesis was that through a process of natural selection more complex species developed from simpler species. The first impulse of churchmen was to reject the theory; it seemed to contradict the Biblical teaching of God's creative activity, the special creation of man, and the plenary inspiration of the Scriptures.

The 1870's witnessed a concerted effort on the part of evolutionists to harmonize their doctrine with the tenets of Christianity. John Fiske argued in his *Outlines of Cosmic Philosophy* (1874), that "evolution is God's way of doing things." About the same time the well-known Scottish evangelical, Henry Drummond, was touring the country with Dwight L. Moody, trying to show that evolution was compatible with dynamic, Christ-centered religion. The rank and file of church members, together with the vast majority of the clergy, however, took their stand against the new ideas and condemned them as destructive of the truth. This opposition was markedly strong in the South, where the state legislatures of Texas, Tennessee, Arkansas, and Mississippi passed laws against the teaching of evolution in public schools.

A major development in the post-war era was the introduction of Biblical higher criticism, which involved a literary-historical study of the Scriptures. During the 1880's, the writings of Julius Wellhausen, a leading German scholar in the Old Testament field, came to be known in the United States. By dating the books of the Bible, Wellhausen discovered an evolution of thought in the Old Testament, starting from polytheistic origins and progressing to ethical monotheism. In the New Testament field similar critical studies were being made by Ferdinand Christian Baur of Tübingen.

Meanwhile, a battery of intellectual forces originating in Europe had begun to beat against the walls of theological conservatism. From the German philosopher-theologian, Friedrich Schleiermacher (1768-1834), came the idea that one finds the living God through an awareness of dependence upon the universe. The basis of authority was shifted from the Bible to the experience of the believer. Philosophically, American thought was shaped by the idealism of Georg W. F. Hegel (1770-1831), reinterpreted for Americans by Josiah Royce (1855-1916). Hegel taught that the universe was inherently rational and that the irrational would eventually be overcome by reason. A third creative force was found in the thought of the German theologian, Albrecht Ritschl (1822-1889). For him religion was intensely practical, its purpose being to cultivate man's innate sense of values. God has shown what man might become in Jesus Christ; it is therefore the task of religion to point men to Jesus.

Certain American thinkers endeavored to fashion these ideas into a theology which would stress the immanence of God in the world and the progressive moral improvement of man. Most of them developed systems which were compatible with evolution and reflective of the new trends in Biblical criticism. Among the important works which shaped the direction of the new theology were *An Outline of Christian Theology* (1898), by the Colgate University scholar, William Newton Clarke; and *Christian Theology in Outline* (1898), by William Adams Brown of Union Seminary, New York.

The new theology bore the obvious imprint of idealistic philosophy. God was to be found in nature, in history, and in the mind and heart of man. In Jesus men could capture their truest insight into the meaning of God and could find an example worthy of emulation. There was place for an Atonement, but not in the orthodox sense of propitiating a just and wrathful God. Rather, Christ offered himself as a living sacrifice in order to show men the love of God and lead them into the larger life of reconciliation with their heavenly Father. As for the concept of man, most liberals regarded him as potentially a son of God; the principal difference between man and Jesus was that the latter more fully realized the potentialities of men than any other. As for the Kingdom of God, it would be achieved not so much by a divine cataclysmic event as by the dedicated service of human beings in the area of social relationships. By following the high example set for them by Christ, men might realize the Kingdom of God on earth. Thus eschatology came to be identified with social ethics.

As denominational leaders confronted the new ideas and made their decisions for and against, controversy swept the churches; in some cases the issues were so hotly contested that ministers were brought to trial for heresy and were disciplined. In no denomination was the conflict waged more fiercely than the Presbyterian, U.S.A. The most publicized case was that of Charles A. Briggs, professor of Biblical Theology at Union Seminary in New York. When he criticized the doctrine of the inerrancy of the Bible in an inaugural address delivered at Union Seminary in 1891, his opponents prosecuted him for heresy before the Presbytery of New York. The case was carried to the General Assembly which, in 1893, decided against Dr. Briggs and suspended him from the ministry.

In various quarters of the Protestant world the theses of liberal theologians would not go unchallenged. Many theological schools, especially those in the Calvinist tradition, produced scholars who were sharply critical of the new currents in religion and clung rigidly to the doctrine of the plenary inspiration of the Bible. In 1895, conservative leaders at the Niagara Bible Conference formulated "five points of fundamentalism" or necessary standards of belief. They were the inerrancy of Scripture, the Virgin Birth of Jesus Christ, the substitutionary theory of the Atonement, the physical resurrection of Christ, and his imminent bodily return to earth. In 1909, two wealthy Californians, Lyman and Milton Stewart, financed the publication of twelve small volumes entitled *The Fundamentals: A Testimony to the Truth*, nearly 3,000,000 copies of which were circulated among ministers and laymen. The effect was to stir up a militant antagonism toward liberalism which would reach its height in the decade following World War I.

While the penetration of higher criticism into the Roman Catholic Church caused serious internal strife in Europe, its effect was considerably less in the United States. The use of historical methodology in Biblical study was not without support among American priests; their thought was not to question dogma but to use the findings of science in support of the church's program. Thus John Zahm of the University of Notre Dame maintained that the evolutionary view of transmutation of species was more devout than the idea of God's immediate creation in six days; few American Catholics, however, were willing to espouse his cause. Leo XIII's critique of "Americanism," in 1899, struck a heavy blow at the liberal movement in the United States. The *coup de grace* came with the issuance of Pius X's encyclical *Pascendi Domini gregis,* in 1907, in which the pontiff specifically condemned modernism and directed that professors tainted with that heresy be dismissed from their posts.

## THE RISE OF NEW CULTS

The cult phenomenon, a distinctive feature of religion in the United States, reached its full flowering in modern, urban, industrial America. A basic contributory force was the voluntary principle, which admitted no state church and encouraged the fullest freedom of religious expression. Equally important factors were the heterogeneity of American society, the competitive impulse in religion, and the spirit of individualism. There were also social and economic considerations. For the poor, crowded into vermin-possessed tenements and forced to lead what seemed an inconsequential existence, some of the cults offered refuge and release. They also provided a haven for those with unfulfilled emotional needs and gave them a sense of belonging and a resuscitated hope for the future.

Various forces contributed to the rise of cults in the late nineteenth century which emphasized the attainment of right states of mind and healing by faith. In 1838, Phineas Parkhurst Quimby (1802-1866), of Portland, Maine, became interested in hypnotism and offered his services to patients, diagnosing their ills and prescribing remedies through the aid of hypnosis. He soon began to experiment with healing through suggestion without the aid of hypnotism. Since disease was merely the result of wrong belief, his remedy for suffering patients was to disabuse them of their errors and plant truth and healing in their place.

One of Quimby's patients was a frail, sickly woman, Mary Baker Eddy (1821-1910), of New Hampshire. In 1862, during an attack from a spinal infection, she placed herself under the care of Quimby and was healed. But according to one of her later statements, it was not until 1866 that she discovered Christian Science and the secret of how to be well. During the next few years, Mrs. Eddy devoted much of her time to the writing of *Science and Health*, the textbook of Christian Science, which was issued in 1875. Four years later she and her followers were granted a charter for the Church of Christ (Scientist), with headquarters in Boston. In 1892, Mrs. Eddy organized the "Mother Church" in Boston as the national church.

Mrs. Eddy found spirit alone to be real and matter to be nothing more than "an image in mortal mind." She defined God, the only reality, as the Trinity of Life, Truth, and Love. The significance of Jesus Christ was that he showed men the way to union with God. Salvation was "Life, Truth, and Love, understood and demonstrated as supreme over all; sin, sickness and death destroyed." Sickness and death were illusions, and sin consisted in regarding them as realities. Such error could be overcome; indeed, the realization of Christian perfection was an ideal possibility to be accomplished by the reception of "truth through flood-tides of love."

After the death of Phineas Quimby, his movement was carried on by Warren Felt Evans and Julius Dresser. The purpose of New Thought, as it came to be known, was "to teach the infinitude of the Supreme one, the Divinity of Man and his infinite possibilities through the creative power of constructive thinking and obedience to the voice of the Indwelling Presence which is our Source of Inspiration, Power, Health and Prosperity." New Thought neither organized as a church nor sought exclusive membership in its groups.

Theosophy is one of those groups which proved attractive to a number of Americans who desired to delve into the mysteries of Eastern religions. It was founded by a Russian noblewoman, Madame Helena Blavatsky, who came to New York in 1873 and established a club which later became the Theosophical Society. Her teachings bore the obvious imprint of Buddhism. In 1906, Annie Besant became president of the society. It was she who provided Theosophy with a systematic presentation of its thought, blending Hindu and Buddhist metaphysics with a Christian moral outlook.

A very different type of cult was the Watch Tower Bible and Tract Society, commonly known as Jehovah's Witnesses. It was founded in 1872 by Charles Taze Russell, who had become convinced from studies of the Bible that the second coming of Christ, in invisible form, would take place in the autumn of 1874. After Russell's death in 1916, leadership of the movement passed to Judge J. F. Rutherford, who became the principal author of its theology. The teaching emphasized the coming theocratic rule of Jehovah over the earth. Jesus Christ, the perfect man and the beginning of God's creation, was God's representative on earth, His appointed emissary to redeem men and establish the Theocracy. Antecedent to the establishment of the Theocracy was the battle of Armageddon and the destruction of evil. The righteous would survive the battle and remain forever on the earth. Then would follow the resurrection of the dead and a thousand-year reign of peace. In recent years the Witnesses have come into conflict with the government over their refusal to salute the flag and their insistence that male members should be recognized as ministers and enjoy exemption from conscription.

# CHAPTER TWELVE

# Social Religion

# in Urban America

One of the marvels of American life in that restless, ebullient era which spanned the administrations of Grant and McKinley was the extraordinary growth of the big cities. In 1870, little more than one-fifth of the country's population lived in urban areas; by 1890, the proportion had risen to one-third. This drive toward the city continued apace until 1910, when it was somewhat offset by a trend to the suburbs. By this time, however, the age of the metropolis had dawned, in which the cities reached out and irresistibly drew the surrounding communities into the vortex of urban life. This influx into the cities was made feasible principally through the rise of great industrial corporations, which, by 1919, were employing 86 per cent of all wage earners.

No social panacea resulted from the trend toward urban civilization. The visitor to a typical East Coast city in 1890, New York for example, would have walked through traffic-congested, litter-strewn streets lined by bleak narrow structures in which "cliff-dwellers" carried on lonely existences in a fellowship of the unconcerned. He might have inspected the grimy tenements, breeding grounds for disease and crime, or he might have looked into the steaming sweatshops where refugees from eastern Europe labored long and dangerous hours for a mere pittance. There were advantages in the city, but there were also hazards and a host of new social problems to be resolved.

Motivated by numerous forces, organized religion sought in varied ways to minister to the social needs of the time. Always to be considered was the activistic spirit of the churches, the desire to be doing something for the Kingdom of God. Also important was the triumph of mass evangelism which nurtured a passion to defeat sin wherever it might appear. Still another factor was the mounting interest in the new psychology and sociology, which sought to deal scientifically with society's problems. Christians were by no means one in their approach to contemporary issues. Some adhered to the pattern of ameliorating social evils by fighting sin and practicing charity; some advocated a reconstruction of economic and political organization along socialistic lines; others were dissatisfied with the social structure but were more conservative in their advocacy of change.

## THE GOSPEL OF WEALTH

The unprecedented fiscal opportunities of the Gilded Age seemed to confirm the view of many that unrestricted personal initiative would lead to rewards commensurate with acumen and industry as well as to maximum economic stability. If theological support for this conviction was sought, it was most likely to be found in the doctrine of God's providence. The most representative apologist for this philosophy was Andrew Carnegie, who presented it in a manner clearly reminiscent of Charles Darwin. As Carnegie propounded the theory in 1889, where there was free competition in business it was inevitable that there should be a higher standard of living. Of course, the process would involve painful social readjustment as the weak gave way before the strong, but the survival of the fittest was the way of life.

A majority of the clergy, while concerned over the problem of mass poverty, carefully avoided any criticism of laissez-faire capitalism and continued to prescribe evangelism as the remedy for social ills. Russell H. Conwell, the most popular lecturer of the day, told his audiences that "money is power and you ought to be reasonably ambitious to have it. You ought because you can do more good with it than you could without it."

During the years of revolutionary economic and social change, a striking transformation took place in the churches. Membership in the large Protestant bodies became almost exclusively the property of professional men, businessmen, white-collar workers, and farmers. While at one time denominations such as the Methodist and Baptist prided themselves on their ministry to the poor, they could now note with satisfaction that they were becoming churches with status, with soaring budgets made possible by millionaire communicants.

With increasing affluence came a demand for external splendor. Gothic and Romanesque structures embellished with beautifully designed stained-glass windows became standard in Protestantism. Some congregations patterned their churches after existing models in Europe, while others sought to outdo them through the achievement of more solid construction and greater beauty.

Church-related colleges also entered into an unprecedented building program made possible by the gifts of philanthropists. Leading universities such as Cornell, Stanford, and Duke originated through the munificent gifts of wealthy industrialists. John D. Rockefeller gave a fortune to the University of Chicago. It was not long before every college in the country was looking for some grand benefactor who would solve all its financial woes.

As churches and colleges looked increasingly to business for support, they came to interpret their own activities more frequently from the standpoint of a business enterprise, emphasizing administration and finance. Successful ministers of large city churches were expected to have all the skills of an oil magnate, while college presidents gave up teaching in favor of administration and fund raising. At denominational conventions there was a tendency to treat the communication of the Gospel much as a corporation might treat the promotion of its product. An aura of professionalism and machine-like perfectionism settled over the churches, leading to the charge that organized religion was becoming concerned more with goals than souls.

## THE LABOR ISSUE

During the 1850's, American labor began to experiment with what came to be a powerful weapon for bargaining with management: the union. While there were only some 300 unions in the country at the close of the Civil War, unionism mushroomed during the ensuing years. One of the more important unions was the Knights of Labor, founded in 1869 to protect workers' rights and advance education and morality. Somewhat more conservative was the American Federation of Labor, a trade-union founded in 1886, which stressed collective bargaining as a means of negotiation.

In September 1873, the nation entered a period of financial depression, hastened by the failure of the leading banking firm, Jay Cooke and Company. Drastic wage cuts brought labor unions into conflict with capital, but the unions were notably unsuccessful. In July 1877, violence broke out between striking railroad workers and militiamen sent to restore order at the Pennsylvania Railroad's Pittsburgh depot. Similar violence in other cities led authorities to take sharp measures against strikers in order to stamp out what appeared to be a labor revolution. In 1886, another series of strikes swept the nation as workingmen agitated for an eight-hour day.

Since the membership of Protestant churches during this period was composed chiefly of persons in the middle class, it is not surprising that ordinarily they failed to see social problems through the eyes of labor. Most were at least nominally concerned over the problem of poverty, but fear of socialism, which they associated with labor, prompted them to oppose the unions.

Nevertheless, an occasional voice spoke in behalf of labor. Episcopal Bishop Frederick Dan Huntington of Central New York admonished his fellow clergy for their indifference to social concerns, and William Jewett Tucker of Andover Seminary maintained that the labor question is a legitimate concern of Christianity. Yet despite the efforts of socially minded Protestant leaders, there was no notable influx of laborers into the churches. A partial explanation for this situation could be found in a statement by Samuel Gompers of the American Federation of Labor in 1898: "My associates have come to look upon the church and the ministry as the apologists and defenders of the wrong committed against the interests of the people, simply because the perpetrators are possessors of wealth . . . whose real God is the almighty dollar."

The Roman Catholic Church had particular reason to be concerned with the problems of labor because much of its membership potential lay in the immigrant labor class. At the same time the church was somewhat embarrassed by the situation, for conservatives within its midst adhered strictly to a policy of non-interference in social issues. Nevertheless, liberals such as Cardinal Gibbons did what they could to abet the cause of labor unions. When Cardinal Taschereau of Quebec obtained from the curia an official disapproval of the Knights of Labor in his province, Gibbons reported to the Prefect of Propaganda that condemnation of the Knights of Labor would have harmful consequences for the church in America. A year later Propaganda ruled that the Knights might be tolerated. Gibbons had won an important victory.

## Christian Social Service

To the impressive number of church members whose social and economic views were of conservative bent, the task of organized Christianity was to provide instruction and worship; for the more unfortunate elements in the community there was the obligation to grant charity and evangelization, since in order to rebuild society one would first have to rebuild men. Firm in this conviction, many Christians inaugurated programs for the amelioration of social conditions.

Among Protestants, the institutional church, designed to render a broader ministry in urban areas, became a standard outlet for the expression of philanthropic concern in the post-Civil War era. St. George's Episcopal Church on the East Side of New York, during the 1880's, opened a parish house and offered courses in industrial education. In Philadelphia, Russell Conwell's Baptist Temple offered gymnasiums, sewing classes, manual-training courses, reading rooms, day nurseries, and social clubs.

Closely related to the institutional church program was the work of the nondenominational city mission. The movement was patterned after the Water Street Mission of New York, founded by Jerry MacAuley, a converted drunkard and burglar, shortly after the Civil War. This rescue mission offered derelicts not only food and shelter but fervid preaching which guided them to reclamation and a life of usefulness. Within a few years many cities had missions of identical character.

After the Civil War, the Young Men's Christian Association began to devote itself increasingly to activities among middle-class youth, particularly to their physical development; in this way bodily exercise became Christianized. For several decades, however, the Y.M.C.A. in certain cities maintained services principally for the poor. In many respects the Young Women's Christian Association, founded in England in 1855 and organized in Boston in 1866, was the feminine counterpart of the Y.M.C.A. While the local associations offered basic services such as providing food and lodging and operating employment bureaus for those in need, their chief emphasis became the cultivation of the "physical, social, intellectual, moral and spiritual interests of young women."

The last twenty years of the nineteenth century witnessed an effort by evangelical Protestants to relate religion to social life through the activities of cooperative organizations such as the Evangelical Alliance and the Convention of Christian Workers. The Alliance brought prominent religious leaders together to discuss the evils of society and seek a solution to them. By 1889, such alliances had been formed in more than forty cities. The Convention of Christian Workers, established in 1886, was an organization of mission workers. Its purposes were to provide classes and reading rooms, to train theological students and laymen in social work, to help individual churches found missions in impoverished areas, and to raise funds for missions.

Prior to 1890, the principal activities of the Roman Catholic Church in the area of social betterment were along charitable lines. One of the most important agencies was the time-honored Society of St. Vincent de Paul, a lay missionary movement which endeavored to bring both physical aid and spiritual sustenance to unfortunates. A leading benevolent fraternal society was the Knights of Columbus, founded for Roman Catholic laymen in 1882. Its original goal was to protect the families of its members by means of a system of insurance; after 1885, the society rapidly developed into a national movement which continued to emphasize beneficence and education.

One of the most remarkable religious and philanthropic organizations was the Salvation Army, founded in England in 1878 by William Booth, a former Wesleyan Methodist preacher. Its program stressed witnessing to Christ by informal preaching and outdoor evangelistic meetings which featured brass bands. After its reorganization along quasi-military lines, the movement became highly centralized and authoritarian. Its theology was conservative, with an accent on sin, redemption, and growth in holiness. The Army was introduced to the United States in 1880; within a few months twelve local units and an official newspaper, the *War Cry,* had been established. The organization was possibly best known for the work of its Slum Brigades, which went into run-down sections of the cities, held services in saloons and halls, brought relief to the destitute, and preached against vice.

## THE SOCIAL GOSPEL

While the main stream of Protestant Christianity in the United States followed a pietistic and doctrinally conservative position which conceived social progress in terms of organized charities, a group of clerical leaders, small at first, began to ask searching questions about the ethics of the social and economic structure of American life. They saw man as a child of God with infinite capacities for moral improvement. They saw Jesus as a prophet of social righteousness. Their Gospel began with men and moved out to God. It was a typically nineteenth-century faith, but one which had been baptized in the life and thought of the Old and New Testaments.

One of the leading voices at the beginning of the Social Gospel movement was that of Washington Gladden (1836-1918), Congregationalist pastor in Columbus, Ohio. He regarded the competitive basis of laissez-faire capitalism as unchristian. A proper goal was cooperation between capital and labor, which would be realized if the worker owned a share in the business. But what was needed most of all in industry was the "power of Christian love." Through the power of love and moral persuasion, a more ideal order was bound to be achieved. Another important contributor was Josiah Strong, Congregational pastor, who stunned the nation by his penetrating analysis of its problems in his book, *Our Country* (1885). It was Strong's contention that greed for money and power was corrupting the country. By sounding a note of crisis, he awakened many ministers and congregations to a vital concern over the social situation and gave a powerful impetus to the cause of the Social Gospel.

Decidedly influential in spreading the Social Gospel was the widely read novel by Charles M. Sheldon, entitled *In His Steps: What Would*

*Jesus Do?* Within a few months after its publication in 1897, one hundred thousand copies had been sold. The story concerned the membership of an average American church and its efforts for an entire year to ascertain and do the will of Jesus in every situation which arose. It was a highly sentimental, romantic account, but it touched the hearts of the public and well nigh brought on a national movement for social reform.

Meanwhile, a ferment of more radical character was welling up under the leadership of an Episcopal clergyman, William D. P. Bliss, who organized a Society of Christian Socialists in Boston in 1889. Insisting that the teachings of Jesus lead inevitably to some type of socialism, the society called for the gradual abolition of competition in business and the introduction of profit-sharing, trade-unionism, and municipal ownership. A vigorous proponent of Christian Socialism was George D. Herron, professor of Applied Christianity at Iowa (later Grinnell) College. The redemptive mission of the church he found to be the erection of a just social order, where the public would own the sources and means of production. This could be accomplished only by willing sacrifice for the interests of others.

The chief prophet of the Social Gospel was Walter Rauschenbusch (1861-1918), German-American Baptist, who adorned the chair of church history at Colgate-Rochester Seminary. Unlike leaders such as Gladden, whose heritage lay in New England Congregationalism, Rauschenbusch was a product of German piety, doctrinal orthodoxy, and social concern in the tradition of Ritschl. He is best known for *A Theology for the Social Gospel* (1917), a frank attempt to find a theological basis for social reform. The author propounded the thesis that it was social sin that was most devastating to morality, whether in the form of war, oppression, or intemperance. Men could not hope to build the Kingdom of God until they made a frontal attack on the Kingdom of Evil. This could come through moral, economic, and social reform, involving the overthrow of capitalism and the establishment of a system not based on a competitive struggle for property and power. As for the progress of the Kingdom, Rauschenbusch was restrained in his optimism; he believed in God's immanence and in progressive perfection but never separated these ideas from his concept of human sinfulness. In this he reflected not so much the thought of his own time as that of a somewhat later time, which was hospitable to Neo-Orthodoxy.

The principal educational center for the heralding of Social Gospel doctrines was the University of Chicago, which featured such celebrated representatives as Albion W. Small, Charles R. Henderson, and Shailer Mathews. Graham Taylor, professor of Christian Sociology at Chicago Theological Seminary, was also well known for his courses on the social teaching of Jesus and his work at the Chicago Commons settlement. Soon a number of seminaries followed the example of Chicago and established chairs in Christian sociology and ethics.

The Social Gospel enterprise met opposition upon its inception from at least two sources. Big business attacked it as a mortal foe and tried unsuccessfully to drive it from the churches. It was also rejected by groups with a strong revivalistic emphasis upon personal redemption from sin. Nevertheless, the movement gradually gained momentum in the great evangelical churches such as the Baptist, Methodist, Congregational, Presbyterian, and Disciples, all of which adopted social creeds and established agencies to put them into practice.

The capstone of the process was the issuance by the newly founded interdenominational body, the Federal Council of Churches, of a Social Creed of the Churches in 1908. This creed, modified by the Council four years later, called for equal rights for all men, child labor laws, laws against the liquor traffic, protection for workers in their places of employment, old age benefits, labor arbitration, reduction of working hours, guaranteed living wages, and "the application of Christian principles to the acquisition and use of property." Thus official ecclesiastical approval was given to a crusade which for more than a generation had been in the process of development. Even so, it seems unlikely that a majority of the laity were won to its cause. With the advent of "normalcy" in the 1920's, the movement declined; more than ten years passed before it enjoyed another revival.

## EXPERIMENTS IN COOPERATION

A salient feature of the American religious enterprise in the late nineteenth century was a trend toward greater cooperation and unity. Estranged families of faith, once given to intercommunal polemics, found it increasingly possible to join forces in a common effort to further the Kingdom of God. Contributory to this development was the growing liberal spirit, which placed more emphasis on a maturing Christian life than on the acceptance of right doctrine. Complex social problems in the great urban areas also seemed to call for the combined efforts of the denominations for a solution. The rapidly expanding world missionary program likewise necessitated a pooling of denominational resources in order to achieve optimum results. To a lesser extent Christian unity was fostered by the community church movement which featured the gathering of local congregations composed of communicants from various denominations but not organically bound to any communion.

With the organization of the Federation of Churches and Christian

Workers of New York City in 1895, a positive step in the direction of interdenominational cooperation was taken. The goal of the Federation was to relate "the gospel to every human need," and to so readjust and direct "its agencies that every family in the destitute parts of our city shall be reached." It was not long before federations with similar purposes were founded in other cities.

Five years after its founding the New York federation called a joint meeting with the Open and Institutional Church League, an organization which had opposed pew rentals and had furthered the work of institutional churches. The result was the formation of a National Federation of Churches and Christian Workers. Local churches and city federations comprised the bulk of its membership. Its inordinate size, however, rendered efficient functioning impossible and suggested the need for a more practical system. Thus at a meeting in 1902, General Secretary Elias B. Sanford called for the establishment of a federation officially endorsed by the denominations. So it came about that the Interchurch Conference on Federation, with official denominational representation, convened in New York in 1905. Out of its deliberations came a plan for the formation of the Federal Council of Churches.

The organizational meeting of the Federal Council of the Churches of Christ in America was held in 1908, the constitution of the new body having already been approved by twenty-eight denominations. Thereafter the Council was to meet quadrennially. Its five objectives were to express the Catholic unity of the Christian Church, to foster cooperative endeavor on the part of the churches, to promote mutual counsel in spiritual matters, to broaden the moral and spiritual influence of the churches, and to encourage the organization of local federations. That the Council appealed to denominations of both liberal and conservative theological orientation was due to the fact that it focused attention on practical problems and refrained from making theological pronouncements.

While the Federal Council was building unity on a national level, various state and city federations unrelated to the Council arranged for interdenominational cooperation within a more limited geographical area. On a city level the federations were usually staffed with an executive secretary and directors of specialized ministries such as Christian Education, the Institutional Ministry, Research and Church Planning, and Social Welfare. Some fifty city federations could boast paid executives on their staffs by 1936; by midcentury the number was even greater. The federations contributed significantly to the work of church planning by arranging for comity agreements among denominations in the establishment of new churches. In the realm of religious education and related fields, both state and local federations often encountered difficulty inasmuch as local churches were ordinarily committed to denominational programs. As the twentieth century progressed, many federations found solutions to this vexing problem and made important gains in the enterprise of interdenominational religious education.

# CHAPTER THIRTEEN

# The Churches

# and World Mission

That deep-seated conviction cherished by Americans that their nation had been divinely chosen for world mission was nurtured and sustained through the fires of civil conflict and given a new baptism of power during the subsequent era. Many forces combined to magnify the role of Manifest Destiny in the American consciousness. Through Darwinism, Americans intuited that by natural selection the United States had become a superior nation destined to rule the weaker peoples of the world. Idealistic philosophies emphasized man's natural ability and interpreted history in terms of progress, a circumstance which had profound implications for expansionists. In a period when European nations were progressively furthering their imperialistic interests in Africa, Asia, Latin America, and the Pacific, Americans too heard the call of benevolent empire and believed their mission to be the extension of the blessings of Christian civilization and democratic government.

## NATIONALISM AND WORLD MISSIONS

The gradually mounting enthusiasm of the churches for missions in the last third of the nineteenth century was a product of national expansionist sentiment combined with deeply embedded theological motives. The desire to save the "heathen" from eternal damnation belonged to the revivalistic spirit which stressed instantaneous conversion and a life directed toward the attainment of perfection. Among many evangelicals the premillennial view that the Gospel would have to be preached throughout the world before the second coming of Christ was a motivating factor. In some instances, missionaries felt an irresistible urge to advance American political and economic interests, believing that in the end all would benefit by American expansion. The result was that through their mission boards the churches poured a steady stream of volunteers into old and new fields of foreign endeavor.

Of particular interest were the missionary gains rendered possible due to changing political situations. In India, after the Sepoy Mutiny of 1857 was finally checked by British arms, the crown took over the government and gave direct support to missionary programs, most of which prospered during the remainder of the century. In China, it was not until the T'ai P'ing Rebellion was brought to a successful conclusion in 1864 that the interior was opened to missionary expansion.

American missions in Korea were made possible after the United States concluded a treaty with the Korean government in 1883. Similarly, diplomatic arrangements preceded organized Protestant missions in Japan. In 1854, Commodore Matthew Perry concluded the first American treaty with the Japanese, thus establishing diplomatic relations between the two countries. After the fall of the Tokugawa Shogunate in 1867, Protestant missions flourished. By the 1890's, however, the churches began to suffer serious losses when a rising tide of nationalism branded Christianity as a foreign religion. Not until the opening of the twentieth century did Christianity enjoy a new period of substantial growth.

Late in the nineteenth century many American Protestant leaders awoke to the possibility of a strong missionary movem nt under the auspices of laymen. This ideal was made concrete in the formation of the Student Volunteer Movement for Foreign Missions in 1888, under the chairmanship of John R. Mott, a lay Methodist. In nations all over the world Student Volunteers were organized to enlist Protestants in the work of missions; through their efforts a high percentage of men destined to become missionary leaders in the twentieth century were recruited. Other lay organizations which initiated world mission activities prio to the end of the century were the Y.M.C.A., the Y.W.C.A., and th Christian Endeavor Society.

To the average American Christian, the extension of national influence and power and the propagation of the faith were but different sides of the same coin. The synthesis to some extent had been achieved by the writings of missionaries, who called for the advance of American political influence in order that backward countries might be saved from native despotism or European imperialism. In something of the same spirit Theodore Roosevelt and Captain Alfred T. Mahan demanded a more powerful navy to promote the imperialistic mercantilism of the nation and to spread superior culture. Roosevelt and Mahan also presented the doctrine, new to Americans, that war was not the worst of evils and might at times be the best means of insuring the triumph of God's righteousness. By 1898, the nation was ideologically prepared for a crusade; its citizenry found it in the Spanish-American War.

During the 1890's, American interest in Cuba was strong, not only for economic reasons but because of its control by the Spanish who were regarded in the United States as cruel obnoxious tyrants. When Spain's harsh colonial policy prompted the Cuban people to rise up against their oppressors, American expansionists in every walk of life became convinced that Cuba should be freed from Spain and brought closer to the American sphere of influence. By 1897, scores of chivalrous patriots were clamoring for war in the name of humanity; the tension mounted, reaching its height with the sinking of the *Maine* in February 1898. Two months later the United States was at war with Spain, with the full blessing of the churches.

The war turned out to be more than a crusade to save the Cubans from corrupt Spain; to most Protestants it also became a divine means of extending their faith to the Philippines and Puerto Rico. They agreed with Senator Albert Beveridge of Indiana that God "has marked the American people as His chosen nation to finally lead in the regeneration of the world." To their complete satisfaction, the United States, after a swift and smashing victory over Spain, gained the Philippines, Puerto Rico, and Guam; Cuba was permitted to set up a republic.

Expansionist policy provided a strong impetus to foreign mission work, enthusiasm for which reached its height in America between 1898 and 1917. The mission enterprise was now popularly conceived to be a patriotic venture. Throughout the country, church benevolences for foreign missions increased by staggering proportions. At the same time there was an unusual change in the motivation behind the mission program. Gone was the stress on rescuing the heathen from eternal damnation. In the light of the new theology, which emphasized the dignity of man and his supreme worth in the sight of God, it seemed somewhat inconsistent to talk of a merciful loving Father sending persons to perdition for not accepting a Gospel they had never heard. Conservative theologians still held to the older view, but they found it poor strategy to hold it too often before the general public. Democratic and humanitarian philosophies, if not as yet successful in creating official modifications of theology, were undoubtedly contributing to the recession of certain concepts such as the idea of eternal damnation, and ecclesiastical leaders were powerless to halt the change in ideology.

Another potent fact was that the missionaries of this period were far less likely to combine religious with imperialistic interests than were their supporters at home. Indeed, in many instances there was open antagonism between missionaries and western merchants who sought to exploit the natives. It was the consensus that businessmen frequently were a hindrance to the missionary program since they created an unfavorable impression of Christianity. It was ironic that these same missionaries should have received so much support from businessmen at home who conceived of missions in a very different light.

Throughout the mission fields the period after 1900 witnessed the growth of interdenominational agencies and increasing recognition of the importance of native leadership. Especially was this true in Japan, the most progressive of the Oriental countries. In 1907, three Methodist missions merged to form the Japanese Methodist Church, which was placed under Japanese control. Four years later, 80 per cent of the native Christians were organized into a Japanese federation of churches. A similar federation was born in India as the result of conferences held in 1909.

## CHRISTIAN IDEALISM IN PEACE AND WAR

At the same time Theodore Roosevelt was presenting his famous justification of war on Christian grounds, advocates of peace were preparing evidence for a rebuttal. During the years immediately following the Spanish-American War, they were conspicuously successful in gaining the support of the American people. The American Peace Society more than doubled its membership. Many denominations regarded it fitting to attack war as uncivilized and unchristian and issued pronouncements to that effect. In 1914, Andrew Carnegie contributed $2 million for the work of the churches toward peace; the funds were administered by the Church Peace Union, a foundation with representatives from Protestant, Roman Catholic, and Jewish bodies. Through a grant from the Union, a conference of delegates from European and American Protestant communions was held at Constance, Switzerland, in 1914, but it was little more than a futile gesture since by this time Europe was being drawn irresistibly into the vortex of war.

Meanwhile, peace enthusiasts in the American churches had for a decade been assuring themselves of the certain triumph of their cause, seemingly oblivious to the ominous rattling of sabers in Central Europe. The tenor of the times was irenic, the national view exultantly optimistic. What was so remarkable about the era was that the impulse toward internationalism was being welded to the campaign for peace, so that America's role as a leader in world affairs was increasingly being seen as that of peacemaker.

This attitude was most evident in the official policy of neutralism with which the United States greeted the outbreak of hostilities in Europe. A steady barrage of allied propaganda, however, evoked from the shocked American public a reaction of contempt for the "German Hun," which was intensified by German submarine attacks resulting in the loss of American lives and by the German refusal to accept President Wilson as a mediator of the peace. By April 1917, Americans had been persuaded that, in the words of their president, "the world must be made safe for democracy," and that the war was not an imperialistic conflict but a crusade for the triumph of good over evil.

In no previous conflict had the American people supported their government with such exuberance as in World War I. Whatever elements of pro-German or neutralist sentiment were still existent by April 1917 were drowned by a vociferous demonstration of patriotism. The rapidity with which the normally independent citizenry adjusted to the demands of a society at war was little short of phenomenal. It was possible because of a deep sense of destiny which propelled them to volunteer for any service they might be qualified to render. There were those who found no sympathy for the war, but they were anathema.

All over the country, patriotic clergymen preached the righteousness of America's cause and exhorted congregations to do their utmost to gain the victory. John Henry Jowett, pastor of Fifth Avenue Presbyterian Church, New York, counseled his people in a sermon preached on January 6, 1918: "Fight to get God's will done! Then the new year in Christ will be a glorious year, the best of all the years, full of life, full of purpose, full of joy, and full of victory." Cardinal Gibbons spoke for his coreligionists in April 1917, when he told a group of newsmen: "The primary duty of a citizen is loyalty to country. This loyalty is manifested more by acts than by words; by solemn service rather than by empty declaration." Newell Dwight Hillis, pastor of Plymouth Congregational Church, Brooklyn, gave evidence of a vindictive spirit when he was moved to remark concerning the German people: "They have no more relation to the civilization of 1918 than an orangoutang, a gorilla, a Judas, a hyena, a thumbscrew, or a scalping-knife in the hands of a savage. These brutes must be cast out of society."

Both the government and the public meted out harsh treatment to opponents of the war. Labor organizations such as the Industrial Workers of the World, which promoted great strikes in the copper mines and lumber camps, felt the full impact of an irate citizenry. There was also much contempt shown for members of pacifist denominations and conscientious objectors. The less than 100 clergymen known to have been pacifists were persecuted for their views.

In a thousand ways the churches boosted morale through activities which ranged from selling Liberty Bonds to entertaining the boys in uniform and knitting socks and sweaters for them. The Federal Council of

Churches founded a General Wartime Commission to coordinate the work of the churches.

Various church-sponsored and nondenominational service organizations ministered in countless ways to military personnel at home and abroad. Next to the Red Cross, the most valuable service agency was the Y.M.C.A. By appointment of the War Department, in 1917, the Y.M.C.A. was commissioned to operate the official canteens and "provide for the amusement and recreation of the troops by means of its usual program of social, educational, physical and religious activities." The efforts of the Knights of Columbus, principally among Roman Catholic soldiers, were similar to those of the Y.M.C.A. Programs for Jewish men in arms were provided by the Jewish Welfare Board and the Young Men's Hebrew Association. The American Bible Society gave away more than a million testaments to fulfill its slogan, "A Khaki Testament in Every Kit."

Despite the fact that the war withdrew from the churches many of their most responsible workers, organized religion suffered no lack of attention or support. Most congregations were beehives of activity and their programs, necessarily modified by the war, featured services by ladies' groups and men who had not been drawn into military service. If their religion was unruffled by winds of doctrine, it did not matter; the Kingdom which they sought would come through the work of their hands, and never were hands busier in laboring for a righteous cause.

As the war progressed, the denominations became more engrossed in plans for the evangelization of the world as soon as the return of peace made that possible. Baptists, Disciples, Methodists, Presbyterians, and other bodies launched great drives to raise funds for world missions. The most grandiose plan was the Inter-Church World Movement, founded at the close of the war in the hope of achieving a federation of evangelical churches and raising a large sum for religious purposes. Essentially it was a five-year plan to consolidate the programs and budgets of the participating denominations. An immense campaign of promotion was undertaken in the assurance that staggering sums would be pledged, but the public wholly failed to respond according to expectation. It was apparent by 1920 that the age of idealism, of crusading internationalism, was rapidly coming to a close. Just ahead lay the erratic years of national introversion, financial boom, and reckless abandon, ending without glory in the silent, lean years of depression.

## Adjustments in Religious Thought and Life

During the brief period of high resolve which followed the war, President Wilson was in France, prepared to commit the United States to the cause of international peace through participation in a League of Nations. But even then forces of reaction at home were undermining his work. In Congress, the Wilsonian dream was subjected to acrimonious repudiation. His health broken, Wilson retired from the national scene and left the stage to Warren Gamaliel Harding and Normalcy.

The 1920's witnessed a drastic change in the relation between society and organized religion. Though the churches flourished, the learned increasingly came to think of them as intellectually inept and smiled with approval at the raging secularism of H. L. Mencken. Far more serious was the fact that religion was gradually losing its power in the lives of men, being patronized but not obeyed. Obvious signs of religion's divorce from the vital issues of life were the decline in family devotions and the casualness with which growing numbers of Americans regarded church attendance. It was not an irreligious age, but vast multitudes managed to live without cultivating more than a nodding acquaintance with religion.

The increasing transience of the population, made more practicable by the automobile, was an important factor in the growing reluctance of Americans to become deeply involved in the life and work of communal organizations such as the church. At the same time the automobile encouraged population movements to suburbs and towns on the fringes of the great cities, leaving downtown areas to business and apartment-hotel dwellers. Most churches in downtown centers were forced to give up all thought of a true parish ministry and become preaching stations. Well-to-do suburbanites were somewhat more likely to participate in parish programs, especially if they had families; they were, however, also highly susceptible to the philosophy that the Sabbath was made for relaxation, and frequently the lure of the open road proved more enticing than the peal of the church bell. Still another type of migration, including poverty-stricken classes such as Negroes moving to the cities of the North and farmers fleeing from the "dust bowl," created unusual problems for organized religion inasmuch as these transients did not adjust easily to their new environments and often abandoned any formal religious connections.

If religion was not in the most robust health, this fact was not revealed by statistical reports. From 1920 to 1930, the percentage of the total population officially numbered as church affiliates rose from 43 to 47 per cent. Religious illiteracy and secularism could increase without affecting growth in church membership, for formal religious affiliation was becoming an accepted feature of American society. Convention was replacing commitment as motivation for membership in the religious community.

Financially, American religious institutions had never been so prosperous. After the brief slump of 1921, American economy enjoyed a steady climb, reaching its zenith in 1929. The churches reaped the full benefits of the era of prosperity. Clerical salaries, long the bane of the ministerial calling, began to improve, while church budgets soared higher with each passing year. Between 1916 and 1926, the value of church property more than doubled.

No denomination made more efficient use of its material resources than the Roman Catholic Church. Of particular importance were the gains made in the area of parochial education. By the late 1920's, 98 per cent of the nation's private elementary schools and two-thirds of its private secondary schools were operated by the Roman Catholic Church.

Concerning worship in the sanctuary, many denominations found themselves in that never-never land which separated the simple, unadorned, didactic rites of Puritanism and pietism from the rich, ceremonial, mystical services of the liturgical churches. Despite a certain distrust of ritualism on the part of low-church conservatives, increasing prosperity and aesthetic sensitivity prompted experimentation in the fine art of public worship. In many instances liberal ministers whose principal attraction was the Social Gospel introduced into their services the ancient hymns and creeds, not because they endorsed their theology but because their use helped to establish a sense of continuity with the universal communion of the faithful in all ages. The trend toward dignity in worship was also reflected in religious architecture. In place of the auditorium-like structures which had once been popular, edifices with a more decidedly religious character were coming into favor.

In the intellectual realm, there was a trend among theologians, whether conscious or not, to become acclimated to the forces of an age which venerated science and found in the philosophy of science its way of life. Christian theology as the exposition of final truth was being progressively neglected by savants in favor of the psychology of religion. The public in general continued, though with growing reluctance, to practice a complacent pietism grounded in a Bible which they respected but did not know.

Philosophy now found itself in the role of judge, armed with a mandate to test the claims of religious authority. After World War I, absolute idealism was unseated from its throne by the empirical theism of William

James (1842-1910) and others, which affirmed the existence of God on the basis that such belief was more satisfactory to the volitional and emotional aspects of man's nature. This God could not be known through dogmatic theology, but only through the human consciousness that the nobler part of man was "continuous with a wider self" which magnified his personality and gave him incentive for creative living. Religion was true because it worked.

A further challenge to complacent religious thinking came from the humanist philosophy of John Dewey (1859-1952). While Dewey rejected the metaphysical God of dogmatic theology, he found a place for a deity which represented the sum of natural forces dedicated to the realization of ideal ends. The purpose of religion was to realize lofty social goals, inspired by experienced values. Only a small percentage of the clergy accepted this teaching; nevertheless, by tearing down the distinction between the sacred and the secular and identifying religion with the social aspirations of man, it contributed to the undermining of orthodoxy.

During the opening decade of the twentieth century, Protestant Fundamentalism, with its famous five points of theological orthodoxy, appeared on the scene in answer to theological liberalism. By 1919, it had gained sufficient strength to warrant the organization of the World's Christian Fundamentals Association, a body pledged to the annihilation of modernist teaching. It was not until the 1920's, however, when a large-scale reaction to secularism and all forms of theological accommodation to it was setting in among Protestants of conservative inclination, that the movement came into its own.

In Tennessee, fundamentalist influence was powerful enough to pressure the state legislature in 1925 to prohibit the teaching of evolution in the public schools. At Dayton, Tennessee, a high-school teacher of biology, John T. Scopes, continued to teach evolutionary views and was arrested. The ensuing trial was farcical, becoming not so much a test of law as a theological debate. On one side was William Jennings Bryan (1860-1925), three-time candidate for the presidency and ardent champion of fundamentalist Christianity, who made an impassioned defense of the Bible as inerrant in matters of science as in faith. Opposing him was the eminent lawyer and agnostic, Clarence Darrow (1857-1938), who presented a sharp ridicule of Biblical literalism and attacked the anti-evolution law as unconstitutional. In the end Scopes was convicted, not because Bryan had disproved evolution, which he had not, but because the defendant had violated an outrageous law.

A widely publicized aspect of the fundamentalist-modernist conflict concerned the position of Harry Emerson Fosdick (1878-    ), a Baptist minister and stated preacher at the First Presbyterian Church, New

York. Liberal in his theological views, he delivered a ringing sermon in 1922 entitled "Shall the Fundamentalists Win?" Conservatives in the denomination brought complaints before the General Assembly; and in 1924, that body invited the controversial minister to enter the Presbyterian Church and subject himself to its discipline or terminate his relationship with First Church. Dr. Fosdick took the latter course and assumed the pastoral leadership of the liberal Park Avenue Baptist Church and later that of the famous Riverside Church, both in New York.

About the same time a controversy was developing in the Presbyterian Princeton Theological Seminary, where Professor J. Gresham Machen was calling for the downfall of liberalism. Though most of his theology was rigidly orthodox, he embraced a doctrine of the church which was unorthodox to Presbyterianism. He held the church to be a voluntary society composed of persons who accepted a common theological position. Growing tension among the faculty led to an official investigation which resulted in a reorganization of the Seminary and the withdrawal, in 1929, of Machen and some of his followers. In 1936, he and his associates organized the Presbyterian Church of America.

The Baptists too were torn by theological dissension. Baptist fundamentalists in the North organized the Fundamental Fellowship of the Northern Baptist Convention in 1920 and attempted in vain to persuade the Northern Baptist Convention to adopt a uniform confession of faith as a safeguard against liberalism. Tension between liberals and conservatives continued to mount until, in 1925, the latter wing founded the Eastern Baptist Theological Seminary in Philadelphia in order to insure the continuation of orthodox leadership. Extreme fundamentalists withdrew from the Convention in 1933 and organized the General Association of Regular Baptist Churches (North).

With the advent of the 1930's, the fundamentalist movement gradually acquired a more negative character, directing its chief criticism toward scholars who denied the plenary inspiration of Scripture. To an era which was feeling the challenge of a dynamic Christo-centric faith, fundamentalism's Bibliocentrism seemed woefully passé. The result was that fundamentalists withdrew into their own spiritual cloister or made their home among the minor sects which offered a mixture of doctrinal conservatism and emotional extravagance.

In no area of the church's total program was the trend toward scientific attitudes more discernible than in the field of education. For some years there had been an emphasis on the improvement of lesson materials and teaching methods in keeping with the newer philosophy of child-centered instruction. An important influence came from the Columbia University educator, John Dewey, who wrote that "the aim of education is the reconstruction and reorganization of experience which adds to the meaning of experience and which increases ability to direct the course of subsequent experiences." Professor George A. Coe of Union Theological Seminary, New York, spelled out the implications of this philosophy for Christian Education. The aim of Christian Education, in Coe's judgment, was the "growth of the young toward and into mature and efficient devotion to the democracy of God, and happy self-realization therein." He rejected the classical view which distinguished between sinful and redeemed man and developed an educational method designed to treat religious experience as a process beginning at birth rather than as a once-and-for-all decision made at the moment of conversion.

The 1920's witnessed a shift by many of the larger Protestant denominations from content-centered to experience-centered curricula. Hand work, construction work, story telling, and purposeful play replaced the older method of simply imparting knowledge of the Bible. Once again religious drama, long repugnant to orthodox Protestantism, came into its own. The guiding spirit behind this development was Fred Eastman, teacher of biography and drama at Chicago Theological Seminary after 1926.

As the larger churches became increasingly concerned with the problems of education, more attention was given to leadership. Many congregations employed full-time Directors of Religious Education who became responsible not only for the program of the Church School but for all youth activities, leadership education, staff retreats, Vacation Bible schools, and countless other educational enterprises. The training of adult laymen in child and youth psychology, in Biblical content, and in administration was numbered among their more important functions.

## Social Religion in the Jazz Age

At no time in American history had formal religious connections been more socially admired and dynamic religious living more casually ignored than in that morbidly gay and effervescent period known as the Jazz Age. Theodore Dreiser mirrored the times in *An American Tragedy,* the story of a youth whose Salvation Army background did not dissuade him from leading a selfish, sensual life. Not even the clergy could escape the agile pen-thrusts of that acrid critic of American society, Sinclair Lewis, as witness his *Elmer Gantry.*

If Dreiser and Lewis were intemperate in their criticisms of contemporary society, it was not because criticism was undeserved. Whether in public or private life there was all too much evidence of scandalous conduct. The weak and ineffectual Harding regime, plagued by such disgraceful episodes as the Teapot Dome scandal, became symbolic of corruption in high places. Yet it was not the flagrantly wicked age that moralists frequently insisted it was. It was an age in transition, recoiling from the drab moralism of the Victorian era and reacting in adolescent fashion to its new-found freedom.

By the 1920's, the idealistic spirit which had favored national prohibition, in the hope of reforming society, was being replaced by a stern righteousness against which every drinker was made to appear an enemy of the social order. If there were those who chafed at the thought of prohibition, it made little difference to moralists. What is important is that there was a reduction in drunkenness, a factor which contributed to a decrease in poverty and an improvement of family relationships. But even the most ardent foes of liquor had to admit that prohibition was not a glorious success; bootlegging was a prosperous industry. At the same time the metropolitan press, essentially anti-prohibitionist, was using its vast resources for molding public opinion to support repeal. Before the advent of the Roosevelt Administration, the Congress initiated the proper constitutional steps and, with approval of the states, the Twenty-first Amendment became law in December 1933, thus bringing prohibition to an end.

An unfortunate concomitant of the return to national insularity was a false "Americanism" inspired by a revival of bigotry and intense fear of every form of radicalism. The year 1919 witnessed a "red" panic brought on by excited reports of communist plots to overthrow the government. The finger of suspicion was pointed indiscriminately at persons of liberal views, and many with alleged communist leanings were prosecuted in the courts.

Simultaneously there was a resurgence of that nativist spirit which identified Americanism with Anglo-Saxon Protestantism and found Roman Catholics, Jews, and sundry aliens from southern and eastern Europe to be a menace to that way of life inaugurated by the founding fathers of the nation. One of the most uninhibited exhibitions of racial and religious bigotry could be seen in the revived Ku Klux Klan, which worked for legislation to prohibit parochial schools, endeavored to gain control of state governments, and fought in 1924 the nomination and in 1928 the election of Alfred E. Smith, Roman Catholic candidate for the presidency on the Democratic ticket.

In 1920, the Federal Council of Churches issued the first in a series of pronouncements against racial discrimination. But segregation remained as firmly entrenched in the churches as in other American institutions. Future progress in this sphere would come largely through social and political action.

During the 1920's, the cutting edge of the older Social Gospel was progressively dulled by the tendency of the churches to emphasize issues such as prohibition, the questionable morality of motion pictures, and the decline of Sabbath observance, and also by the failure of socially concerned organizations such as the Federal Council of Churches to do more than reiterate the basic ideals which they had been promulgating for years.

Immediately after World War I, a group of business executives endeavored to break the power of labor unions through the organization of an "Open-Shop Movement." Though this unsuccessful strategy was widely condemned by Christian leaders, the fear that labor unions were in league with Russian Communists gave rise to a popular antagonism toward labor. In the case of the U.S. Steel Strike (1919), the Interchurch World Movement and the Federal Council of Churches conducted an investigation, the former body issuing a report sympathetic to labor's demand for an eight-hour day to replace the then current twelve-hour working day. As a result the two organizations were bitterly assailed by management and accused of radicalism. The strike was crushed, but support for labor began to increase among Protestants who read the report. The National Catholic Welfare Council and the National Council of Rabbis also called for reform. Their voices were heard; by 1923, the twelve-hour day for steel workers was a thing of the past.

At the same time powerful ideological forces were preparing a rebuttal to the pro-labor argument. One came from the well-known writer, Bruce Barton, who tried to convince the public in his best-selling biography of Jesus entitled *The Man Nobody Knows* that Jesus was the founding father of advertising and business, a veritable executive concerned with the problems of management. A far more influential argument, coming largely from the laity, was that Christian ethics had no relevance to social problems and the churches should confine their declarations to theological matters. While there was little that laymen could do to curb the social pronouncements of ecclesiastical dignitaries, they could and did bring a halt to the preaching of the Social Gospel in their parishes. "Big Business" was enthroned in the churches and professing Christians worshipped before the altars of material prosperity. Then, in a moment, the Jazz Age, the age of normalcy, was over and a sorely chastened America struggled through stormy years of poverty and war at whose end there was no rainbow.

# CHAPTER FOURTEEN

# Religion

# in an Era of Crisis

Like a thief in the night came the Great Depression, leaving behind it a nation in the throes of panic and poverty. It worked its wrath on all classes and conditions of men—rich and poor, young and old, male and female—and drew them irresistibly into the fellowship of suffering and despair.

## RELIGION AND THE DEPRESSION

Religious institutions felt the full impact of the financial collapse, particularly by 1932. Many congregations which had contracted heavy debts for building programs during prosperous times had to face the bitter fact of foreclosure. Collections dropped almost 50 per cent from 1930 to 1934; in urban areas this invariably meant a sharp cut in ministerial salaries, while in the rural parishes it frequently necessitated dispensing with full-time pastoral services for the remainder of the crisis. Religious attitudes toward the disaster were varied. Protestants in general regarded it as a punishment for sins. Fundamentalists found it to be a sign of the imminent second coming of Christ. Roman Catholic interpreters usually emphasized the remedial function of current suffering and pointed to the eschatological hope of a better life in the world to come.

Many religious leaders supposed that hard times would cause Americans to make a fresh scrutiny of their spiritual needs and seek out the ordinances of religion. Their hopes did not see fulfillment. Between 1930 and 1940, the churches gained at only one-half the percentage rate of the previous ten-year period. In 1940, membership in all religious bodies was reported at 64,501,594 or 49 per cent of the nation's population. While these figures may be correct, they denote at best a nominal membership and reveal nothing concerning the spiritual pulse of a people. The spirit of secularism had in no wise diminished and the decline in regular church attendance proved it.

Only among the extremely evangelistic Protestant groups were there evidences of phenomenal gains during this period. The secret of their attractiveness was unquestionably in offering the financially distressed a better life in that glorious world which would be established with the return of Christ. Particularly successful were the Pentecostal and Holiness sects, which presented a strongly revivalistic message in a decade which was experiencing a dearth of revivals.

During the early years of the depression, the churches did what they could to minister to the needs of the suffering through the time-honored method of charity, but without notable success. Thus when the Roosevelt Administration began to take positive social action, the churches hailed the step forward and promptly curtailed their efforts to provide relief. By 1935, the nation was well along the road to economic recovery.

## Religion in an Era of Tension and War

The rise of Hitler to power in 1933 and his subsequent invasion of the Rhineland, Austria, and Czechoslovakia, together with Japan's aggressions in China, brought deep concern to many thoughtful Americans. Despite governmental efforts to maintain neutrality, it was clear that it was just a matter of time before the United States would be drawn into the chaos of war. Reluctantly the nation began to arm for defense.

While church organizations generally approved the Lend-Lease program for aid to friendly nations, adopted by Congress in 1941, the decision in 1940 to draft men into military service was greeted with loud cries of protest. Pacifist Christians could support a program of material assistance to beleaguered nations, but they were inalterably opposed to any action which appeared to be a step toward actual participation in conflict. Gradually the cleavage in the churches over this issue widened. At the very time several of the denominations were petitioning President Roosevelt to keep the nation out of war (1941), a group of churchmen headed by Reinhold Niebuhr sought to counteract the pacifist influence.

Pearl Harbor decided the issue. After that, many of the churches which had fought intervention issued resolutions in support of the war effort. Throughout the nation religious people greeted the conflict not as a glorious crusade, but as a cross which had to be borne if the world was to know any semblance of peace and justice.

If the institutions of religion could not bless the war as holy, they could and did throw the weight of their support behind the national effort to gain a victory as quickly as possible and with the least loss of life. One of the most important ways by which they ministered to the men and women in uniform was through the provision of chaplains. In the autumn of 1940, the government announced a policy of providing one chaplain for every 1,200 men in army service. The principal work of the chaplains was to conduct services of worship and patriotic exercises, provide classes for religious instruction, and act as counselors to service personnel. There was frequently close cooperation between the chaplains of the various faiths, a circumstance which fostered tolerance and understanding.

Social and recreational activities were provided for servicemen by the government, with the assistance of Christian and Jewish benevolent agencies. Recreation buildings were staffed by the United Service Organizations which coordinated the work of the Y.M.C.A., the Y.W.C.A., the National Catholic Community Service, the Salvation Army, the Jewish Welfare Board, and the National Travelers' Aid Association. Part of the duties of these organizations was to make available religious guidance for those who desired it.

Though many church bodies gave their official blessing to conscientious objectors, only about one per cent of all registrants sought that classification. These persons were ordinarily assigned to non-combatant service in work camps. By the end of 1944, about 8,000 men were working in forty-seven Civilian Public Service Camps supervised by the Selective Service System.

The war had not long been under way before the churches turned to the all-important task of laying the groundwork for a lasting peace. As early as March 1942, the Federal Council of Churches' Commission to Study the Bases of a Just and Durable Peace, chaired by John Foster Dulles, issued a report which called for "a continuing collaboration of the United Nations." In November 1942, the National Catholic Welfare Conference called for the "establishment of an international order in which the spirit of Christ shall rule the hearts of men and of nations." The following month the American Institute of Judaism proposed the foundation of a world council of Christianity and Judaism to work for the establishment of righteousness and brotherhood in the post-war age.

When the war finally drew to a close in 1945, the religious institutions of the United States became more actively engaged in the furtherance of their international responsibilities. The use of the atomic bomb in order to shorten the war with Japan, they recognized, placed upon their nation the duty to give moral leadership in the area of atomic power. Another responsibility was that of caring for and rehabilitating suffering peoples in war-torn lands.

It was perhaps inevitable that the churches should have devoted more emphasis in their international programs to practical relief, health, and education. The evangelistic motive was less in evidence, in large measure because indigenous churches in former mission territory had assumed the function of caring for the spiritual needs of their countrymen. What was distressing to missionary leaders in the United States was the decline in prestige of Christianity in many countries at a time in which nationalism and communism were making rapid strides.

Sensing that the achievement of world peace depended in large measure upon an effective international organization, American religious bodies gave overwhelming endorsement to the formation of the United Nations. A declaration by the Federal Council of Churches in March 1946 was representative: the "United Nations offers a hopeful procedure whereby governments can peacefully adjust their disputes and advance their common interests."

Despite the efforts of peace-loving countries to promote good feeling, the United Nations was swept from one international crisis to another during the first unpropitious decade of its existence. Most serious were the cold war between the communist and free worlds and the hot war in Korea, instigated by North Korean aggressors in June 1950. Though the authority of the United Nations was vindicated by the intervention of the United States and other member powers, the war was unpopular among Americans. Most citizens admitted that intervention was unavoidable but were appalled by the magnitude of the sacrifice and the indecisive nature of the conflict, which dragged to its formal close in 1953. As for the powers of organized religion, the war prompted them to intensify efforts in behalf of world peace, particularly through the development of a sense of community.

## MOVEMENTS TOWARD CHRISTIAN UNITY

During the years which separated World War I from the midcentury, the trend toward religious cooperation and cohesiveness, already in evidence for several decades, continued with certain marked results. There were a number of important mergers between denominations which sprang from common roots and enjoyed similar beliefs and organization. Among the more notable of these were the unions of the Lutheran General Synod, the General Council, and the United Synod of the South (1918), to form the United Lutheran Church in America; the Methodist Episcopal Church, the Methodist Episcopal Church, South, and the Methodist Protestant Church (1939), to form the Methodist Church; the Presbyterian Church in the U.S.A. and the United Presbyterian Church of North America (1958), to form the United Presbyterian Church in the U.S.A.; the Evangelical Lutheran Church, the American Lutheran Church, and the United Evangelical Lutheran Church (1960), to form the American Lutheran Church; and the American Unitarian Association and the Universalist Church of America (1961), to form the Unitarian Universalist Association.

An even more striking evidence of the growing desire for union was the consummation of several mergers between denominations of different heritage and tradition. In 1931, the Congregational Churches united with the Christian Church, a product of the New Light movement of the early nineteenth century, to form the Congregational Christian Churches. Lutheran and Reformed traditions were mingled in the Union of the Evangelical Synod of North America and the Reformed Church in the United States in 1934 to form the Evangelical and Reformed Church. In 1957, this body consummated a union with the Congregational Christian Churches, thus constituting the United Church of Christ. The most noteworthy feature of the merger was that it brought together denominations which had been governed by modified Presbyterian and Congregational polities.

With the nascence of the Federal Council of Churches there developed simultaneously certain interdenominational federations of mission boards or other administrative agencies of the churches. These were the Foreign Missions Conference of North America, the Home Missions Council of North America, the International Council of Religious Education, the National Protestant Council of Higher Education, the Missionary Education Movement of the United States and Canada, the United Stewardship Council, and the United Council of Church Women. These federations merged with the Federal Council in December 1950, to form the National Council of the Churches of Christ in the United States of America. This was a remarkable step forward in interchurch cooperation, for it placed under the care of a single agency all phases of interdenominational activity.

Most noteworthy during this period was the development of the ecumenical (from the Greek word *oikoumene,* meaning the inhabited world) movement, which may be defined as that process whereby Christian communions in every part of the world strive to discover and express a common faith and life centered in commitment to Jesus Christ, their redeeming Lord. It received an early impetus in the World Missionary Conference, convened in Edinburgh in 1910. It was carried forward in conferences on Faith and Order at Lausanne, Switzerland (1927), and Edinburgh (1937), and on Life and Work at Stockholm (1925) and Oxford (1937).

At a meeting in London in 1937 of representatives from the various branches of the ecumenical movement, plans were made for the creation of a single body which would unite the work of the various movements without infringing on their independence. A constituent Committee was appointed to draw up a constitution for the proposed World Council of Churches. This document, sent to the churches in 1938, provided for admission to membership of all communions which accepted Jesus Christ as God and Saviour. August 1941 was set as the date for the convening of the Assembly of the World Council, but by that time World War II had broken out and the Assembly had to be postponed indefinitely.

After a long delay the World Council of Churches convened at Amsterdam in August 1948. Its 351 official delegates represented 147 churches in forty-four countries. There were no representatives from the Roman Catholic or Russian Orthodox Churches, and two large American denominations, the Southern Baptist Convention and the Lutheran Missouri Synod, refrained from sending delegates. Fundamentalist churches proceeded to found a rival organization known as the International Council of Christian Churches. Still the World Council was the most comprehensive Christian body yet to assemble, with representation from all five continents.

The main theme for discussion was "Man's Disorder and God's Design." Though there was general agreement concerning basic Christian principles, certain conflicts appeared. The principal debate was between John Foster Dulles, American Presbyterian layman, and Josef L. Hromadka, Czech theological professor, over capitalism and communism. Still, the Assembly was an overwhelming success and did much to further the cause of Christian unity.

The Second Assembly of the World Council was held at Evanston, Illinois, in August 1954. A record number of 502 delegates officially represented the 163 member communions throughout the world. The central theme for deliberation was "Christ—the Hope of the World," a subject which called forth sharp differences in theological viewpoint. European theologians found their hope in the Saviour Christ, whose work was to call men out of the world and prepare for them a new creation. American theologians, on the other hand, placed more emphasis on ethics than eschatology as popularly interpreted to mean the "doctrine of the last things." The Assembly found it impossible to reach any real unanimity as to the meaning of "Christian Hope" or eschatology. The result was a report which found room for both points of view. Probably the most important contribution of the Assembly was the effect which it had upon the world. Few gatherings in modern times have received such attention; unquestionably, thousands were heartened by the spirit of unity which existed in the face of diversity.

## TRENDS IN RELIGIOUS THOUGHT AND EDUCATION

If theological liberalism had emerged triumphantly from the conflict with fundamentalism during the 1920's, it did not have long to glory in its victory. Already forces were being released which would prove destructive of the radiant idealism and evolutionary meliorism. The American might naturally tend to be an optimist, but he found it difficult to maintain that condition in an era which witnessed such a series of calamities as the failure of the League of Nations, the depression, World War II, the Korean War, and the mounting threat of communist aggression. Gradually he began to give consideration to the disastrous consequences of personal sin and to some extent develop an experiential awareness of his own guilt.

Most significant for religious philosophy was the importation of existentialism from Europe. This system, which came to be known in America primarily through the work of the nineteenth-century Danish thinker, Sören Kierkegaard, struck at the roots of idealism with its tragic picture of human life estranged from God. Out of it grew theologies which stressed the sinful nature of man's action, his utter need of divine grace, his personal encounter with the living God, and God's gift of salvation.

The first important manifestation of theological existentialism in America came through the crisis theology of the Swiss Protestant theologian, Karl Barth (1886-    ). In his commentary on Romans (1919), he startled his readers by introducing them to a God who confronts man in a demand for his decision to accept or reject the divine will. This God speaks to man through Jesus Christ alone; He speaks in a moment of crisis, an existential moment, in which man's sin stands uncovered and he responds to the divine will humbly in an act of total commitment. This dynamic encounter is possible only through faith which is a gift of God. It was not until the late 1920's that Barthian theology began to make a vital impression on American thinkers.

The primary revisionist and interpreter of existentialism in the United States was Reinhold Niebuhr (1892-    ) of Union Theological Seminary, whose *Moral Man and Immoral Society* (1932) constituted a clarion call for theological and social reconstruction. From studying the New Testament and observing the savage struggles for power in society, Niebuhr concluded that Jesus' ethic was one which demanded perfection and was therefore impossible of attainment. It stood in judgment over every ethical situation and summoned the Christian to recognize his moral inadequacy and seek forgiveness. Niebuhr's concept stood between Barthianism, which saw the Kingdom of God only as a future hope, and American liberalism, which confused the Kingdom with human progress. For Niebuhr the Christian way was to work for every possible reform, recognizing the difficulty of moral progress but trusting that each task performed in faith would have significance in the unfolding of the divine purpose.

By the mid-1930's, a new theological era was in the making. Harry Emerson Fosdick, dean of liberal preachers, dramatized the change in 1935 in his provocative sermon, "The Church Must Go Beyond Modernism," delivered at Riverside Church. Fosdick's indictment of modernism was that it had placed too much emphasis on intellectualism, that it had been overly sentimental, that it had humanized the concept of God, and that it had conformed too much to the standards of the modern world. The time had come for Christians to stand apart from the "prevailing culture" and challenge it.

But if there were changes they were not all in the direction of Barthianism. There was also developing a school which might be termed neo-liberal. Its position was clearly delineated by John C. Bennett of Union Seminary, who maintained that the best in liberalism should be preserved and integrated with the best in orthodoxy. Thus the liberal views that man is essentially good and that he is responsible for his thoughts and deeds were indispensable. It was also important to realize that sin is real and ever present in society, that a utopian order cannot be achieved on earth though some progress may be expected, and that repentance is constantly necessary to save men from the sins of pride and self-righteousness.

Among the distinguished theologians who were indebted to both liberalism and neo-orthodoxy, mention may be made of H. Richard Niebuhr, Robert L. Calhoun, and Walter M. Horton. Niebuhr, of Yale Divinity School, stressed the sovereignty of God and the grace of Jesus Christ as necessary in the redemption of society and the need for the Christian movement to be revolutionary and dynamic. His colleague, Calhoun, held similarly to a religious realism gripped by neither radical pessimism nor uncritical optimism. Horton, of Oberlin Graduate School of Theology, adopted a liberal evangelicalism. His theology stressed God as personal and transcendent and religion as redemptive; while it admitted the possibility, even the probability, of tragedy in human history, it found that history is moving toward the fulfillment of God's purpose.

By the 1950's, there were signs of a resurgence of strength among right-wing conservatives. Under the leadership of such thinkers as Edward

J. Carnell and Carl F. H. Henry, they presented a more rational and philosophical defense of their faith and demonstrated a willingness to enter the wider arenas of theological discussion.

Possibly the most creative thinker among Protestant theologians was Paul Tillich (1886-    ), German emigré who taught at Union Seminary from 1933 to 1954, thereafter becoming professor at Harvard University. For Tillich, theology begins with the problem of fallen man, with man's ultimate concern which determines his being or non-being in relation to God who is Being itself. The central problem of life is to find the courage to be, to participate in the ultimate power of being. Christian theology deals with this problem in its presentation of Christ as the center and meaning of history, as the means whereby man finds the answer to his existential self-estrangement and meets God in a dynamic encounter.

Tillich found the heart of religion in the Biblical message of justification by faith, the paradox that sinful man is accepted by God as if he were righteous. With the realization that God has accepted him as he is, man can overcome his feelings of guilt and anxiety and his pretentiousness and can confront the ambiguities of life without rationalizing them away. Protestantism must bear witness to this free grace of God which points men beyond themselves and must protest against any inclination to place either dogma or the church in the place of God. Any giving of one's ultimate concern to that which is not ultimate, such as the state or the church, is idolatrous. One's ultimate concern must be the living God.

The period also witnessed, at least on the popular level, a renewed interest in the Bible. This interest was evidenced in the number, quality, and popularity of the more recent translations, especially the Revised Standard Version (1946 and 1952). In the area of Biblical study, a commission of leading Protestant scholars issued a twelve-volume commentary known as *The Interpreter's Bible* from 1951 to 1957.

The awakening of interest in Christian theology during the 1930's contributed to a changed emphasis in the entire program of Christian education. The trend was to produce lesson materials for the church' school which placed more emphasis on theology and on the relevance of the Bible for contemporary living.

With the reemphasis on theology came a recovery of the communal aspects of the Christian life, notably the church as a divine fellowship, the significance of the Christian home, and the importance of a close relationship between religious guidance in the home and in the church school. New denominational curriculums issued during the late 1940's and 1950's included material specifically for parents and helps for family worship and education as well as lessons for Sunday classes. Along with the trend toward family-centered programs came a growing stress on the recruitment and training of lay staffs to carry on the many and varied duties of religious education. In numerous cities local federations of churches joined with neighborhood congregations in offering content and methods courses for training teachers and prospective teachers.

## SOCIAL RELIGION IN A TIME OF READJUSTMENT

While the 1930's witnessed a revolt from the older "Social Gospel" liberalism, there was no concomitant departure from a sense of social responsibility. What was lost was the buoyant optimism born of the conviction that through man all things were possible. What was gained was a fresh awareness of the depths of human pride and passion. The result was a renewed zeal to relate God's will to the social order as far as this was possible in a society embroiled in the struggle for power and addicted to the absolutizing and deifying of its own relative interests. Despite this manifest transformation, the churches found it difficult to recapture the standing in a secular society which they had held prior to the 1920's. It was an age of increasing secularism, outwardly respectful to religion but patently indifferent or unconcerned.

The single besetting problem of American society in the era of crisis was race. An awakened Negro minority, increasingly aware of its rights and opportunities, was insisting that the "separate but equal facilities" principle was unjust and was making demands for legislation on behalf of public integration. In 1946, the Federal Council of Churches admonished its member churches to work for a "nonsegregated society." Several denominations took similar action. In many cases Roman Catholic and Protestant clergy met defiance from their membership when they called for integration. Certainly there were relatively few congregations which functioned on an integrated basis. The decision of the United States Supreme Court in 1954 that racial segregation in public schools was unconstitutional created tension in some quarters. But most Americans acquiesced in changes which they knew to be inevitable and prayed for wisdom to guide them through a difficult period of adjustment.

By the 1920's, the right of women to vote and to participate in public life had been assured. After that time a number of communions permitted women to serve on local or national boards. In regard to ordination the denominations were more conservative, though by 1959 women might be ordained in such bodies as the American Baptist, the Disciples of Christ, the United Church of Christ, and the United Presbyterian in the U.S.A.

The assimilation of Jewish immigrants into the environment brought with it profound changes in Jewish life and thought. Socially, there had been a steady rise in status on the part of the east-European group during the second and third decades of the century. With material advancement, however, came an alarming indifference toward the traditional faith, especially on the part of the younger generation. In many cities the Jewish Center became the chief expression of "Jewishness," providing a specifically Jewish orientation for cultural activities. Religion figured in the community movement, but only as one among many expressions of "Jewishness." The most receptive of the three Jewish bodies to this trend was Conservatism.

For centuries the Zionist hope that Jewish nationality would one day be restored in Palestine was a cardinal feature of Jewish religion. It was not, however, until the period of World War I that Zionism assumed the character of a mass movement in the United States; by 1930, nine national Zionist groups had been organized. As a result of the mass persecution of Jews by Hitler and anti-Jewish violence in Arab countries during the 1930's and 1940's, thousands of American Jews began to contribute to or work for the United Jewish Appeal or the Zionist organizations.

After World War II, there was a revival of Judaism as a religion and a concomitant decline in zeal for the principle of "Jewishness." During the 1950's, there were evidences of increased attendance at services and a greater inclination to observe the religious customs and ceremonies. These changes were undoubtedly linked to contemporary patterns of religiousness in American culture.

From the beginning of the national era, the constitutional provision that Congress shall make no laws respecting a religious establishment was broadly interpreted to imply the separation of church and state; actually no separation existed in an absolute sense inasmuch as churches were tax exempt and chaplaincies existed in Congress and the military services. During the twentieth century there was considerable agitation on the part of the Roman Catholic Church to have the traditional view of "separation" modified so that the church might receive additional benefits from the government.

The Roman Catholic policy was indicated in a manifesto issued in 1948 by the American bishops, who called for "free cooperation between government and religious bodies—cooperation involving no special privilege to any group and no restriction on the religious liberty of any citizen." The following year the noted theologian Father John Courtney Murray disavowed any inclination on the part of his church to seek a union with the state. On the other hand, John A. Ryan and F. J. Boland's work, *Catholic Principles of Politics* (1943), caused many Americans to question the church's permanent support of the separation principle.

One issue of primary concern was the reestablishment of diplomatic relations with the Vatican. In 1939, President Roosevelt decided to send Myron C. Taylor as his personal representative to the pope. Though Taylor was not considered a member of the regular diplomatic service, many feared that his appointment constituted a step toward the opening of formal diplomatic relations. A number of Protestant communions protested the appointment, but it remained in effect until 1950 when Mr. Taylor voluntarily resigned.

Another problem concerned religious education in conjunction with the public school system. As early as 1913, a program of week-day religious instruction was inaugurated at Gary, Indiana, whence it spread to other states. Known as the "released-time" plan, it permitted a certain amount of time to be taken from the regular school day in order that pupils might attend classes taught by teachers provided by churches and synagogues.

In 1945, the legality of "released time" was questioned by Mrs. Vashti McCollum in a suit before the Sixth Illinois Circuit Court. She maintained that the system led to discrimination against her son, who took no classes in religion and was mocked by the children who did. When she lost the decision, she carried the case to the United States Supreme Court, which ruled in 1948 in favor of Mrs. McCollum.

Another important issue concerned the allocation of any tax revenues for the direct or indirect benefit of parochial schools. After World War II, the Roman Catholic hierarchy, consistently committed to the expenditure of state funds for parochial schools, intensified its efforts to obtain state benefits for its sectarian educational institutions. Some of the concessions made in certain localities included free textbooks of a nonreligious nature, free hot lunches, and free school-bus transportation. Certain states were willing to employ as teachers in the public schools nuns who wore the distinctive garb of their order.

One of the bitterest disputes over federal aid to parochial schools concerned a bill introduced by Congressman Graham Barden of North Carolina in 1949. It provided that federal funds should be granted only to public schools. When Mrs. Franklin Roosevelt came out in favor of federal aid to public schools only, Francis Cardinal Spellman of New York assailed her as "anti-Catholic." His attack brought down such a flood of public criticism as to cause the red-faced cardinal to issue a more temperate statement. The encounter was but symbolic of a burning issue in American society which promised to become more intensified with the passage of time.

## SPIRITUAL IMPULSES AT MIDCENTURY

The years which followed Hiroshima and Nagasaki were troubled by international tensions and anxieties which harassed the spirits of the American people. Confronted by a Russian leviathan which blew alternately hot and cold, Americans could never entirely dismiss from their minds the dread prospect of a future war ending in the obliteration of mankind. Everywhere the cry went out for security and came back like a hollow echo from the abyss. Nevertheless, Americans refused to abandon wholly their essential inclination toward optimism, believing implicitly that they could find a panacea in the ordinances of religion.

By almost any materialistic standard American religious institutions were becoming increasingly robust. For more than a decade church attendance continued to swell, as a mass of frustrated, confused, and depressed but still hopeful people looked to religion for reassurance and happiness. Among Protestant bodies in particular there was renewed emphasis on evangelism and a number of denominations initiated special programs for the enrichment of spiritual life in the parishes. All over the country there was a rising tide of lay religion, and under the influence of the Quaker philosopher, Elton Trueblood, and others, greater importance was attached to the ministry of the laity.

Sunday-morning services were patronized to such an extent that many churches were obliged to offer a duplicate "early" service. To the average church attendant the Sunday service became the principal hour, possibly the only hour, of weekly inspiration. He came to expect from it not primarily a learned homily but fellowship with the divine and some "practical" word of guidance to help him meet the day-to-day problems of life. As a consequence there developed a revival of worship as a primary means of spiritual enrichment.

The period also saw a marked growth in the utilization of wider avenues of communication by the churches. After 1923, leading radio networks granted free time to ecclesiastical organizations for the production of non-polemical programs of inspiration. During the 1950's, television developed into a useful medium of religious communication. In addition to telecasts of religious programs on Sunday mornings, there were numerous special network presentations such as Bishop Fulton J. Sheen's weekly series and the Billy Graham revival meeting in New York. Motion pictures also became an important means of spreading religious knowledge.

Mass revivalism, ineffectual since the days of Billy Sunday, came once again into popular favor. Traditional in its zeal for the salvation of souls, it was at the same time contemporary in its opposition to secularism, communism, and moral relativism. Its ability to relate the Gospel to the search for peace of mind or to the problem of juvenile delinquency was prerequisite to an effective and beneficial witness. The movement had its beginnings in the Youth for Christ revivals at the outset of World War II.

Most popular and ostensibly successful of the contemporary revivalists was William (Billy) Franklin Graham (1918-    ), Baptist minister. In 1947, he launched a series of evangelistic campaigns which took him to the major cities of the nation. At the New York crusade in 1957, in which Graham reached the apex of his evangelistic career in America, 56,767 persons made decisions for Christ. Using all the customary techniques of a professional revivalist, Graham presented his listeners with a compelling but simplified pietistic Gospel which emphasized individual salvation through decision and public profession of one's faith in Christ. He gave little if any evidence of social discernment and certainly made no effort to relate the Gospel to the highly complex problems of contemporary society. On the whole the Graham revivals appealed to the great middle class rather than to the very rich or extremely poor and constituted a rally for that segment of the population which tended most to be identified with formal religion.

Concomitantly came the national quest for peace of mind. The trend began as early as 1946 with the publication of Rabbi Joshua Liebman's best seller, *Peace of Mind,* a primer of religious psychology which pointed the way to newness of life through mental discipline. Other versions of how to attain peace soon followed with Fulton J. Sheen's *Peace of Soul* (1949) and Billy Graham's *Peace with God* (1953). The recognized leader of the "cult of reassurance," however, was Norman Vincent Peale (1898-    ), popular minister of the Marble Collegiate (Reformed) Church in New York City, who sought through his preaching and writing to help people find a simple technique to the fine art of living. His solution, which appealed to thousands of anxious citizens who viewed religion as a source of "practical" help, was to blot out negative thoughts and turn for guidance to the Bible, to Christ, to prayer. Critics attacked him for the superficiality of his theology; but after all, he was addressing himself to a non-theologically oriented public which conceived religion primarily as a stepping-stone to mental and physical health, happiness, and prosperity.

Ironically, when the "peace-of-mind" cult was at the crest of its popularity in the early 1950's, America was gripped by a wave of hysteria brought on by fear of communism. McCarthyism was abroad in the land and investigating committees were busily engaged in ferreting out information which might link some distinguished citizens to the communist conspiracy. Even members of the clergy whose loyalty was upheld in the end were exposed to "smear" tactics.

Meanwhile, the trend to religion had continued unabated; by the early 1950's, the new piety had permeated every quarter of American life. At no time in the nation's history was religion treated with such approbation, scepticism with such scorn. The secular press heralded the return to piety, while motion pictures and popular songs with a quasi-religious theme enjoyed unprecedented popularity. President Dwight D. Eisenhower symbolized the spirit of the times with his simple and unaffected piety; millions were moved beyond words by the sincerity of the brief prayer which he offered on the occasion of his first inaugural.

Everywhere there was talk of a religious revival sweeping the nation. Uncritical products of the culture accepted it just as they accepted practically everything else in an increasingly standardized society. Religion belonged to decent American living; any other thesis was unpatriotic. The precise nature and form of religion seemed relatively unimportant except to an unconventional minority which required definition for its faith. What was essential was "belief," whatever its character. Thus thousands adhered to little more than a simple, nondescript faith of sentimentalities, with an anthropomorphic theology which pictured God as little more than a kindly Santa Claus or "the man upstairs."

Various analyses of the current religious situation have been forthcoming. Some have interpreted it as the victory of secularism through identity with religion. Others have linked it to the rise of a national cult which has developed coextensively with a trend toward conformity and standardization, the result being all too often the absolutizing of relatives and the relativizing of absolutes. The emerging religion has been characterized by some as humanistic nationalism. Its deity ministers to a people who have no sins, only anxieties.

Granted that there have been evidences of secularism and humanistic nationalism as powerful ideological factors in American religious life, it is equally true that there have been intelligent and dedicated efforts to bring life in a disordered world into conformity with the dynamic will of that Supreme Being who is the Lord of history.

Among many persons of spiritual depth and creativity there has been a mounting conviction that the central religious problem which faces Americans at the dawn of the Atomic Age is inexorable bondage to a sanctified world of man-made absolutes. These concerned individuals stand convinced that Americans must not fashion that kind of world. They voice the conviction that above the relativities of history abides the living God, whom to know is life and whom to love is perfect freedom. They cannot identify America with the Kingdom of God, but they trust that in spite of human fallibility they can work for its coming.

# Suggested Reading

## GENERAL WORKS

Among the more important cultural and social treatments are N. M. Blake, *A Short History of American Life* (McGraw-Hill Book Co., Inc., 1952); A. M. Schlesinger and D. R. Fox, eds., *A History of American Life*, 13 vols. (The Macmillan Company, 1927-1948); and H. S. Commager, *The American Mind* (Yale University Press, 1950). For a splendid collection of documents illustrative of religious life see H. S. Smith, R. T. Handy, and L. A. Loetscher, eds., *American Christianity*, Vol. I (Charles Scribner's Sons, 1960). A general historical study of religious movements and institutions may be found in C. E. Olmstead, *History of Religion in the United States* (Prentice-Hall, Inc., 1960).

## CHAPTER ONE: THE OLD WORLD HERITAGE

Able interpretations of the Reformation period may be found in R. Bainton, *The Reformation of the Sixteenth Century* (Beacon Press, 1952); H. J. Grimm, *The Reformation Era. 1500-1650* (The Macmillan Company, 1954); and P. Janelle, *The Catholic Reformation* (The Bruce Publishing Co., 1949). A. C. McGiffert gives a comprehensive account of Protestant theology in *Protestant Thought before Kant* (Charles Scribner's Sons, 1936). The status of Judaism is discussed in S. Grayzel, *Through the Ages; The Story of the Jewish People* (Jewish Publication Society of America, 1947).

## CHAPTER TWO: CHURCH AND EMPIRE IN COLONIAL AMERICA

The missions of New Spain and New France are treated in H. E. Bolton, *The Spanish Borderlands: A Chronicle of Old Florida and the Southwest* (Yale University Press, 1921); H. I. Pricstlcy, *The Coming of the White Man* (The Macmillan Company, 1929); G. M. Wrong, *The Rise and Fall of New France*, 2 vols. (The Macmillan Company, 1928); and J. H. Kennedy, *Jesuit and Savage in New France* (Yale University Press, 1950). Colonial Anglicanism is discussed in W. F. Craven, *The Southern Colonies in the Seventeenth Century, 1607-1689*, Vol. I, *A History of the South* (Louisiana State University Press, 1949); W. W. Manross, *A History of the American Episcopal Church* (Morehouse-Gorham, 1950); and Chapter II of W. W. Sweet, *Religion in Colonial America* (Charles Scribner's Sons, 1949). Helpful summaries of religion in New Netherland and New Sweden may be found in C. M. Andrews, *The Colonial Period of American History*, Vol. III, *The Settlements* (Yale University Press, 1937); and A. Johnson, *The Swedish Settlements on the Delaware*, 2 vols. (University of Pennsylvania Press, 1911).

## CHAPTER THREE: PURITAN BEGINNINGS IN NEW ENGLAND

Outstanding works by Perry Miller are: *Orthodoxy in Massachusetts, 1630-1650* (Harvard University Press, 1933); *The New England Mind, The Seventeenth Century* (Harvard University Press, 1954); and *The New England Mind, From Colony to Province* (Harvard University Press, 1953). Also valuable are A. Simpson, *Puritanism in Old and New England* (University of Chicago Press, 1956); and O. Winslow, *Meetinghouse Hill, 1630-1783* (The Macmillan Company, 1952). A fine collection of primary materials may be found in P. Miller and T. Johnson, *The Puritans* (American Book Company, 1938).

## CHAPTER FOUR: RELIGIOUS DIVERSITY IN THE ENGLISH COLONIES

For the development of Roman Catholicism in Maryland see T. Maynard, *The Story of American Catholicism* (The Macmillan Company, 1943). Excellent biographies of Roger Williams are P. Miller, *Roger Williams* (The Bobbs-Merrill Company, Inc., 1953); and O. Winslow, *Master Roger Williams: A Biography* (The Macmillan Company, 1957). The work of William Penn is ably described in C. O. Peare, *William Penn* (J. B. Lippincott Co., 1957); and F. B. Tolles and E. G. Alderfer, *The Witness of William Penn* (The Macmillan Company, 1957). General studies of colonial Presbyterianism include M. W. Armstrong, L. A. Loetscher, and C. A. Anderson, *The Presbyterian Enterprise* (The Westminster Press, 1956); and L. J. Trinterud, *The Forming of an American Tradition* (The Westminster Press, 1949). See A. R. Wentz, *A Basic History of Lutheranism in America* (Muhlenberg Press, 1955); and P. A. Wallace, *The Muhlenbergs of Pennsylvania* (University of Pennsylvania Press, 1950) for the German Lutheran bodies.

## CHAPTER FIVE: THE GREAT AWAKENING

The Middle Colony Revival is discussed in C. Maxson, *The Great Awakening in the Middle Colonies* (University of Chicago Press, 1920). A fine interpretative analysis of the New England revival may be found in E. S. Gaustad, *The Great*

*Awakening in New England* (Harper & Brothers, 1957). Leading works on Jonathan Edwards are P. Miller, *Jonathan Edwards* (William Sloane Associates, Inc., 1949); and O. Winslow, *Jonathan Edwards, 1703-1758* (The Macmillan Company, 1940). For the revival in Virginia see W. M. Gewehr, *The Great Awakening in Virginia* (Duke University Press, 1930). Theological trends are cited in H. S. Smith, *Changing Conceptions of Original Sin* (Charles Scribner's Sons, 1955).

## CHAPTER SIX: RELIGION AND THE BIRTH OF A NATION

The standard works are E. F. Humphrey, *Nationalism and Religion in America, 1774-1789* (Chipman Law Publishing Co., 1924); C. H. Van Tyne, *The Causes of the War for Independence* (Houghton Mifflin Company, 1922); A. M. Baldwin, *The New England Clergy and the American Revolution* (Duke University Press, 1928); A. P. Stokes, *Church and State in the United States,* Vol. I (Harper & Brothers, 1950); and W. W. Sweet, *Religion in the Development of American Culture* (Charles Scribner's Sons, 1952).

## CHAPTER SEVEN: CHURCH EXPANSION AND THE SECOND AWAKENING

A good account of America's geographical expansion may be found in R. A. Billington, *Westward Expansion* (The Macmillan Company, 1949). W. W. Sweet summarizes church expansion in *Religion in the Development of American Culture.* General accounts of the missionary enterprise are given in K. S. Latourette, *The Great Century,* Vol. IV, *A History of the Expansion of Christianity* (Harper & Brothers, 1941); and J. R. Bodo, *The Protestant Clergy and Public Issues* (Princeton University Press, 1954). For a brief account of the Second Awakening see B. A. Weisberger, *They Gathered at the River* (Little, Brown & Co., 1958).

## CHAPTER EIGHT: PATTERNS OF RELIGIOUS DIVERSIFICATION

Transcendentalism and the rise of Unitarianism and Universalism receive scholarly treatment in W. R. Hutchison, *The Transcendentalist Ministers* (Yale University Press, 1959); E. M. Wilbur, *A History of Unitarianism,* 2 vols. (Harvard University Press, 1945-1952); and C. P. Wright, *The Beginnings of Unitarianism in America* (Starr King, 1955). For theological developments in Congregationalism consult S. E. Mead, *Nathaniel William Taylor, 1786-1858* (University of Chicago Press, 1942); and B. M. Cross, *Horace Bushnell* (University of Chicago Press, 1958). The rise of the Disciples' movement is surveyed in W. E. Garrison and A. T. DeGroot, *The Disciples of Christ* (Christian Board of Publication, 1948); and D. R. Lindley, *Apostle of Freedom* (The Bethany

Press, 1957), a biography of Alexander Campbell. H. S. Smith treats the theological conflict between Old and New School Presbyterians in *Changing Conceptions of Original Sin*, Chap. 6. German Reformed theology is discussed in L. J. Binkley, *The Mercersburg Theology* (Franklin & Marshall, 1953).

## CHAPTER NINE: SOCIAL REFORM IN AN AGE OF CONFLICT

Ante-bellum movements of evangelism and reform are discussed in T. L. Smith, *Revivalism and Social Reform* (Abingdon Press, 1957); J. L. Peters, *Christian Perfection and American Methodism* (Abingdon Press, 1956); A. F. Tyler, *Freedom's Ferment* (University of Minnesota Press, 1944); C. C. Cole, Jr., *The Social Ideas of the Northern Evangelists, 1826-1860* (Columbia University Press, 1954); and J. R. Bodo, *The Protestant Clergy and Public Issues*. Useful discussions of the slavery controversy may be found in E. L. Fox, *The American Colonization Society, 1817-1840* (The Johns Hopkins Press, 1919); G. H. Barnes, *The Anti-Slavery Impulse, 1830-1844* (Appleton-Century-Crofts, Inc., 1933); and W. S. Jenkins, *Pro-Slavery Thought in the Old South* (University of North Carolina Press, 1935). Important general works related to the Civil War which touch on the history of religion are A. C. Cole, *The Irrepressible Conflict, 1850-1865* (The Macmillan Company, 1934); and E. M. Coulter, *The Confederate States of America, 1861-1865*, Vol. VII, *A History of the South* (Louisiana State University Press, 1950).

## CHAPTER TEN: CHURCH EXTENSION AND CONSOLIDATION

Able accounts of the churches and the Negro are W. E. B. Du Bois, *Black Reconstruction* (Harcourt, Brace & Company, 1935); and W. D. Weatherford, *American Churches and the Negro* (Christopher, 1957). The religion of the immigrant is discussed in G. M. Stephenson, *The Religious Aspects of Swedish Immigration* (University of Minnesota Press, 1932); C. E. Schneider, *The German Church on the American Frontier* (Eden, 1939); G. Shaughnessy, *Has the Immigrant Kept the Faith?* (The Macmillan Company, 1925); and J. Higham, *Strangers in the Land: Patterns of American Nativism, 1860-1925* (Rutgers University Press, 1955). For Judaism and Eastern Orthodoxy see N. Glazer, *American Judaism* (University of Chicago Press, 1957); and C. W. Emhardt, *The Eastern Church in the Western World* (Morehouse-Barlow Co., Inc., 1928).

## CHAPTER ELEVEN: RELIGIOUS LIFE IN THE VICTORIAN ERA

In W. E. Garrison, *The March of Faith* (Harper & Brothers, 1933), there is a good general treatment of religious life. The resurgence of revivalism is discussed in B. A. Weisberger. *They Gathered at the River*. New trends in theology and Biblical studies are reviewed in F. H. Foster, *The Modern Movement in*

*American Theology* (Fleming H. Revell Co., 1939); and H. S. Smith, *Changing Concepts of Original Sin.* Among the better studies of religious cults are M. Bach, *They Have Found a Faith* (The Bobbs-Merrill Company, Inc., 1946); and C. S. Braden, *These Also Believe* (The Macmillan Company, 1950).

## CHAPTER TWELVE: SOCIAL RELIGION IN URBAN AMERICA

For the churches and labor see H. F. May, *Protestant Churches and Industrial America* (Harper & Brothers, 1949); and H. J. Browne, *The Catholic Church and the Knights of Labor* (The Catholic University of America Press, 1949). Christian social service is described in A. I. Abell, *The Urban Impact on American Protestantism, 1865-1900* (Harvard University Press, 1943). Good discussions of the Social Gospel may be found in C. H. Hopkins, *The Rise of the Social Gospel in American Protestantism, 1865-1915* (Yale University Press, 1940); and D. R. Sharp, *Walter Rauschenbusch* (The Macmillan Company, 1942). Movements toward church unity receive careful study in C. S. Macfarland, *Christian Unity in the Making* (Federal Council of Churches, 1948).

## CHAPTER THIRTEEN: THE CHURCHES AND WORLD MISSION

The history of missionary expansion is treated in K. S. Latourette, *The Great Century in the Americas, Australasia, and Africa,* Vol. V, *A History of the Expansion of Christianity* (Harper & Brothers, 1943) and *The Great Century in Northern Africa and Asia,* Vol. VI in the same series (Harper & Brothers, 1944). For the churches and World War I consult A. P. Stokes, *Church and State in the United States,* Vol. III; and R. H. Abrams, *Preachers Present Arms* (Round Table Press, 1933). Various phases of religion during the 1920's are interpreted by N. F. Furniss, *The Fundamentalist Controversy, 1918-1931* (Yale University Press, 1954); H. E. Fosdick, *The Living of These Days* (Harper & Brothers, 1956); P. A. Carter, *The Decline and Revival of the Social Gospel* (Cornell University Press, 1954); and R. M. Miller, *American Protestantism and Social Issues, 1919-1939* (University of North Carolina Press, 1958).

## CHAPTER FOURTEEN: RELIGION IN AN ERA OF CRISIS

A general work of considerable value is H. W. Schneider, *Religion in 20th Century America* (Harvard University Press, 1952). For a study of the Depression see S. C. Kincheloe, *Research Memorandum on Religion in the Depression* (Social Science Research Council, 1937). Religion in a period of global conflict is treated in A. P. Stokes, *Church and State in the United States,* Vol. III. In the field of Christian unity the definitive history is R. Rouse and S. C. Neill, *A History of the Ecumenical Movement, 1517-1948* (The Westminster Press, 1954). A number of important books deal with reconstruction in religious thought, among them C. F. H. Henry, *Fifty Years of Protestant Theology*

(W. A. Wilde Co., 1950); A. S. Nash, ed., *Protestant Thought in the Twentieth Century* (The Macmillan Company, 1951); D. W. Soper, *Major Voices in American Theology* (The Westminster Press, 1953), and *Men Who Shape Belief* (The Westminster Press, 1955). Trends in social religion are charted in P. A. Carter, *The Decline and Revival of the Social Gospel*; and R. M. Miller, *American Protestantism and Social Issues, 1919-1939*. A. P. Stokes discusses issues of church and state in *Church and State in the United States*, Vol. II. For penetrating analyses of the contemporary religious situation consult R. E. Osborn, *The Spirit of American Christianity* (Harper & Brothers, 1958); M. E. Marty, *The New Shape of American Religion* (Harper & Brothers, 1959); and "Religion in American Society," *The Annals of the American Academy of Political and Social Science* (November, 1960).

# Index

Fitzgerald, Edward, 108
Flaget, Benedict Joseph, 65
Forty-two Articles, of Church of England, 3
Fosdick, Harry Emerson, 141-142, 153
Fox, George, 5, 32-33
Franklin, Benjamin, 42, 48
Frelinghuysen, Theodore, 41
French and Indian War, 10, 50
Friends, Society of: in colonial America, 15, 17, 32-34; in the national era, 65, 98; origin of, 5
Frontier. See Western expansion
Fundamentalism, 120, 141-142, 151

Garrison, William Lloyd, 94-95
German Reformed Church: in colonial America, 40; in the national era, 80
Gibbons, James, 108-109, 126, 137
Gladden, Washington, 128
Gough, John B., 91
Gould, Thomas, 31
Graham, William (Billy), 159
Greek Orthodoxy, in the United States, 110

Half-Way Covenant, 25
Harby, Isaac, 84
Harding, Warren G., 139
Hegel, Georg W. F., 119
Henderson, Charles R., 129
Henry VIII, of England, 3
Henry, Carl F. H., 154
Herron, George D., 129
Higginson, Francis, 22
Hillis, Newell Dwight, 137
Hobart, John Henry, 80
Hodge, Charles, 80, 95
Holiness. See Perfectionism
Hopedale Community, 86-87
Hopkins, Samuel, 47-48, 68
Horton, Walter M., 153
Hromadka, Josef L., 151
Hudson, Henry, 16
Humanism, modern, 141
Humanitarianism: and the first revival, 47; pre-Civil War, 91-96
Hunt, Robert, 11
Huntington, Frederic Dan, 126
Huss, John, 38

Immigration: in the colonial era, 11, 13-18, 20-21, 27-28, 32-35; in the pre-Civil

War era, 81-82; in the post-Civil War era, 106-108, 110-111
Indians, American: attitude of colonists toward, 8-11, 13, 18, 24-25, 30, 34; and western expansion, 69, 105
International Uniform Lessons, 115

Jackson, Sheldon, 105
James I, of England, 3, 11, 19-21
James II, of England, 13, 28
James, William, 140-141
Jarratt, Devereux, 46
Jefferson, Thomas, 48, 52, 55
Jehovah's Witnesses, 122
Jogues, Isaac, 10
Joliet, Louis, 10
Jones, Samuel P., 115
Jowett, John Henry, 137
Judaism: in colonial America, 17; in the national era, 84-85, 109-110, 155-156
Judson, Adoniram, 70

Kierkegaard, Sören, 152
King, John, 46
Kirk, Edward N., 92
Knights of Columbus, 127
Knights of Labor, 125-126
Korean War, 149
Ku Klux Klan, 144

Laud, William, 21
Lee, Ann, 86
Leeser, Isaac, 84-85
Leland, John, 82
Leo XIII, Pope, 109, 120
Lewis, Sinclair, 143
Liebman, Joshua, 159
Lincoln, Abraham, 100
Louis XIV, of France, 38
Louisiana Purchase, 62
Lovejoy, Elijah, 95
Loyola, Ignatius, 6
Luther, Martin, 2, 37
Lutheran Church: in colonial America, 18, 38-39; in the national era, 58-59, 83-84, 98, 106-107; origin of, 2

McCabe, C. C., 104-105
McCarthyism, 159-160
McCollum, Mrs. Vashti, 157
Machen, J. Gresham, 142
McIlvaine, Charles, 81
Mahan, Alfred T., 134

# SPECTRUM  PAPERBACKS

*Other SPECTRUM Books . . . quality paperbacks that
meet the highest standards of scholarship and integrity.*

## Classics in History Series